Syllable in the City

PostNet Suite #41
Private Bag x7
Parkview
Johannesburg
South Africa
2122

Text copyright @2024 Martha van Zyl
Copyright Syllable in the City
Cover art by Kobus Bam

Martha van Zyl has asserted her right to be identified as the author of this work.

All rights reserved.
No part of this publication may be reproduced, stored in or into a retrieval system or transmitted in any form or by any means (electronic, mechanical, photocopying, recording, or otherwise) without the prior written permission of the copyright owner.

ISBN: 978-0-7961-4455-3
BISG: CKB13000 | SPO028010

Just a ginchident

When F1 and cocktails collide

Compiled by Martha van Zyl

For Morné, Andrea, and Grant. I'll never be able to thank you enough.

Contents

Introduction

Glassware

Mixology equipment

Cocktail syrups

Lights Out Punch

Lewis Hamilton

Sergio Perez

Pierre Gasly

George Russell

Alex Albon

Oscar Piastri

Yuki Tsunoda

Zhou Guanyu

Daniel Ricciardo

Fernando Alonso

Nico Hülkenberg

Valtteri Bottas

Carlos Sainz Jr

Esteban Ocon
Max Verstappen
Kevin Magnussen
Charles Leclerc
Lance Stroll
Lando Norris
Logan Sargeant
Testing, testing
Bahrain
Saudi Arabia
Australia
Japan
China
Miami
Italy (Imola)
Monaco
Canada
Spain
Austria
United Kingdom

Hungary
Belgium
Netherlands
Italy (Monza)
Azerbaijan
Singapore
COTA
Mexico
Brazil
Las Vegas
Qatar
Abu Dhabi
Acknowledgements
Index of gins
Index of cocktails

Introduction

Sundays are for gin and F1. Well, this year also a few Saturdays. So, I've decided to collect some of my favourite gin cocktails for the circuits and drivers.

I started watching F1 in the early 2000s with my first roomy, Morné. Or rather, I'd watch the race start, fall asleep, and somehow wake up in time to see the chequered flag. Eventually, I got better at staying awake and engaged, and I loved Ferrari and Kimi Räikkönen from the start.

Long story short, I moved back home and stopped watching F1 until I started dating former racing hottie Grant. About a year before I met Grant, the small batch gin movement took South Africa by storm, and my work friend turned real friend Andrea went on the gin journey with me.

Early in the 2022 season, Valtteri Bottas and Tiffany Cromwell launched a gin, and I was desperate to get my hands on it. However, it was not to be (yet). However, this planted the seed of matching drivers and circuits with cocktails. And naturally, it would have to be gin cocktails. So, here we are.

Unless otherwise indicated, the recipes yield one standard drink.

These drinks are mixed in the Southern Hemisphere but can be enjoyed universally. Most of the gins recommended with each recipe are South African craft gins. Those not from SA are indicated with an asterisk *

Please drink responsibly, whether you do so in celebration or commiseration.

Cheers!

Martha x

Birthday 11 December 19**
Nationality South African
Favourite circuit Kyalami
Favourite driver Kimi Räikkönen
Favourite cocktail French 75
Favourite local gin Mother's Ruin
Favourite international gin Hendrick's

@themarthamyth
@syllcity

Glassware

Presentation is everything and it's important to serve your cocktail in the appropriate glass. The size, shape, and style impact the visual perception and enjoyment of the drink. These are a few classic glasses to have in your collection.

Martini glass

The most iconic of all cocktail glasses, the conical martini glass emerged with the art deco movement. The long stem is perfect for chilled drinks as it keeps people's hands from inadvertently warming the cocktail.

Highball glass

Sometimes also known as a Collins glass, these glasses are perfect for serving drinks with a high ratio of mixer to spirit. The highball glass is versatile enough to be a substitute for similarly shaped glasses like the zombie glass.

Lowball glass

The lowball glass, also known as a rocks or old-fashioned glass, is a short, squat tumbler and is great for serving any spirit on the rocks or for short mixed cocktails.

Champagne flute

The tall, thin flute's tapered design reduces the champagne's surface area to help keep the fizz in the drink for longer.

Shot glass

This glass is a home bar essential and can hold just enough spirit to be drunk in one mouthful. It also has a firm base that can be satisfyingly slammed on a bar top. The shot glass can also stand in for a measure when making cocktails.

Margarita glass

The margarita glass, our coupette was designed specifically for margaritas. It is ideal for any frozen blended drinks.

Hurricane glass

This pear-shaped glass pays homage to the hurricane lamp and was the glass used to create the New Orleans rum-based cocktail, the Hurricane. It is also used for various frozen and blended cocktails.

Sling glass

This is design classic used to serve the Singapore Sling and the Long Island Iced Tea. The tall body and short stem make it ideal for chilled drinks.

Mixology equipment

The equipment you have in your home bar depends on your mixology level. These are the essential tools of the trade.

Measures and jiggers

A jigger is a bartender's basic measuring tool and essential for crafting the perfect blend of ingredients. Look for a steel jigger with clear markings so you can easily and accurately pour measures.

Bar spoon

A proper bar spoon has a small bowl and a long handle that allows you to muddle, mix, and stir with ease. Spoons come in various lengths and widths, and a stylish bar spoon is an attractive addition to any bartender's kit.

Shaker

Most contemporary shakers are made from steel since it doesn't tarnish or easily conduct heat. In addition, most standard shakers come with a built-in strainer. However, if you're using a Boston or Parisian shaker, you'll need to use a separate strainer.

Muddler

For mashing up fruit or crushing herbs, a muddler is essential. It is a chunky wooden tool with a rounded end and can also be used to make cracked ice.

Strainer

A bar strainer is essential to prevent ice and other ingredients being poured into your glass. Some cocktails need to be double strained, so even if there's a strainer in your cocktail shaker, you'll still need a separate Hawthorne strainer.

Other equipment

You might consider adding a juice, citrus peeler, sharp paring knife, etc. in your arsenal of mixing tools.

Cocktail syrups

A simple syrup is a staple to sweeten cocktails and comprises equal parts water and granulated sugar. From here, you can create endless variations. And if you prefer a sweeter sweetener, create a rich simple syrup by changing the ratio to one part water to two parts demerara sugar.

Once sealed and refrigerated, your simple syrup has a one-month shelf life.

Remember to mark your different syrups clearly to ensure you get the right flavour for your cocktail.

Heat the water and sugar in a small saucepan over medium heat and stir until the sugar is completely dissolved.

Let it cool and pour it into a clean glass bottle with a lid.

For honey syrup, simply replace the quantity of sugar with the same of honey.

To make cucumber syrup, add 10 cucumber slices to your simple syrup and leave them until the syrup cools completely. Then, discard the cucumber.

Add a sprig or two of rosemary to your simple syrup as it cools. Discard the rosemary when bottling your syrup.

Pomegranate syrup:
200 g pomegranate seeds
400 g castor sugar
20 mint leaves
500 ml raw cider vinegar

Muddle the pomegranate seeds, sugar, and mint in a medium bowl. Cover and refrigerate for 24 hours to macerate. Remove from the fridge, stir in the vinegar, cover again, and let it stand for another 24 hours. Strain through a muslin cloth before storing.

Spiced syrup:
900 ml water
900 ml sugar
5-cm piece of fresh ginger chopped
2 makrut lime leaves
5 ml rosewater
6 cracked cardamom pods
2 cracked lemongrass stalks
10 mint leaves

Bring the ingredients to a simmer in a pot over medium heat and steep for an hour. Chill the syrup, strain through a cheesecloth, and discard the solids. Refrigerate in an airtight container for up to two weeks.

Rose petal syrup:
Petals from five pesticide-free roses
4.5 cups of granulated sugar
Gently clean petals by swirling in a bowl of cold water.
Drain on paper towels.
Bring five cups of water, the sugar, and petals to boil in a medium-sized saucepan.
Remove from heat and steep covered for an hour.
Pour through a fine sieve and let cool.

Chai syrup
15 green cardamom pods
1 cinnamon stick
1 star anise pod
5 allspice berries
3 cloves
2 cups sugar
2 cups water

Gently crush the cardamom pods with a mortar and pestle or the flat edge of a chef's knife.

Place the cardamom pods, cinnamon stick, star anise pod, allspice berries, and cloves on a baking sheet.

Toast for 5 minutes in the oven ate 180°C.

Heat the water and sugar in a saucepan until the sugar dissolves.

Add the toasted spices and allow to simmer for 10 minutes.

Let the syrup cool before straining out and discarding the solids.

The syrup will keep for up to a month if tightly sealed and refrigerated.

Ginger simple syrup

1 cup sugar

1 cup water

½ cup peeled and chopped ginger

Stir the sugar and water in a small saucepan over medium heat until the sugar is dissolved.

Remove from heat add the ginger, allowing it to steep, covered, for at least 20 minutes.

Strain and discard the solids.

Refrigerate for up to two weeks in a tightly sealed container.

Lights Out Punch

This isn't a gin cocktail, but it's the perfect way to kick off the year. And if you don't know why, you need to educate yourself quicksmart.

Don't be put off by the grocery list of ingredients. It's as simple as combining everything at least the day before.

Serves 12 - 16.

1 ½ tablespoon spiced black tea leaves
350 ml sweet vermouth
750 ml reposado tequila, chilled
350 ml apple juice or cider, chilled
230 ml lemon juice, freshly squeezed
120 ml rich demerara syrup, chilled
16 dashes of Angostura bitters
700 ml soda water, chilled

Combine the tea leaves and vermouth in a jar and set aside for 90 minutes before straining and refrigerating. If you don't have tea leaves, I'm sure you can steep two teabags in the vermouth.

Pour the tea-infused vermouth, tequila, apple juice, lemon juice, demerara syrup, and bitters into a punch bowl. Stir to combine, then add the soda water.

Garnish the punch bowl generously with apple slices and cinnamon sticks.

Serve in punch cups or mugs and add an apple slice and cinnamon stick if you want.

And away we go!

Championship Records

Number of WDC Titles

Michael Schumacher 7
Lewis Hamilton 7
Juan Manuel Fangio 5
Alain Prost 4
Sebastian Vettel 4

Number of Constructor's Titles

Ferrari 16
Williams 9
McLaren 8
Mercedes 8
Lotus 7

Lewis Hamilton

Birthday 7 January 1985
Nationality British
Race number 44

First race Australia 2007
Drivers' titles 7
Podiums 197

Tom Collins

Lewis gave up alcohol a few years ago, so this is a non-alcoholic version of a classic, for a classic.

I was tempted to pair #44 with a Gibson, given Lewis' aversion to onions. He can't bear to touch them – it's like a cat seeing a cucumber.

60 ml alcohol-free gin
30 ml lemon juice
15 ml simple syrup
Soda water
Ice

This mocktail requires no special tools and is built in a highball glass over ice and garnished with a lemon slice.

Recommended: Seedlip Grove 42*.

Sergio Perez

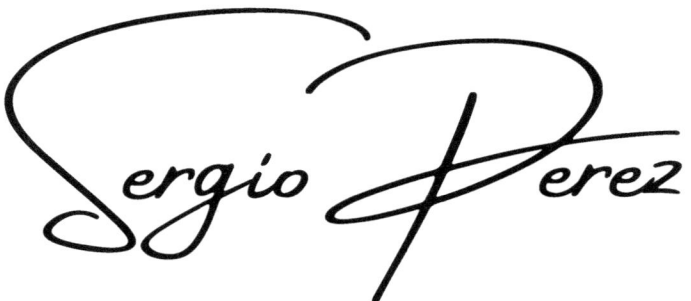

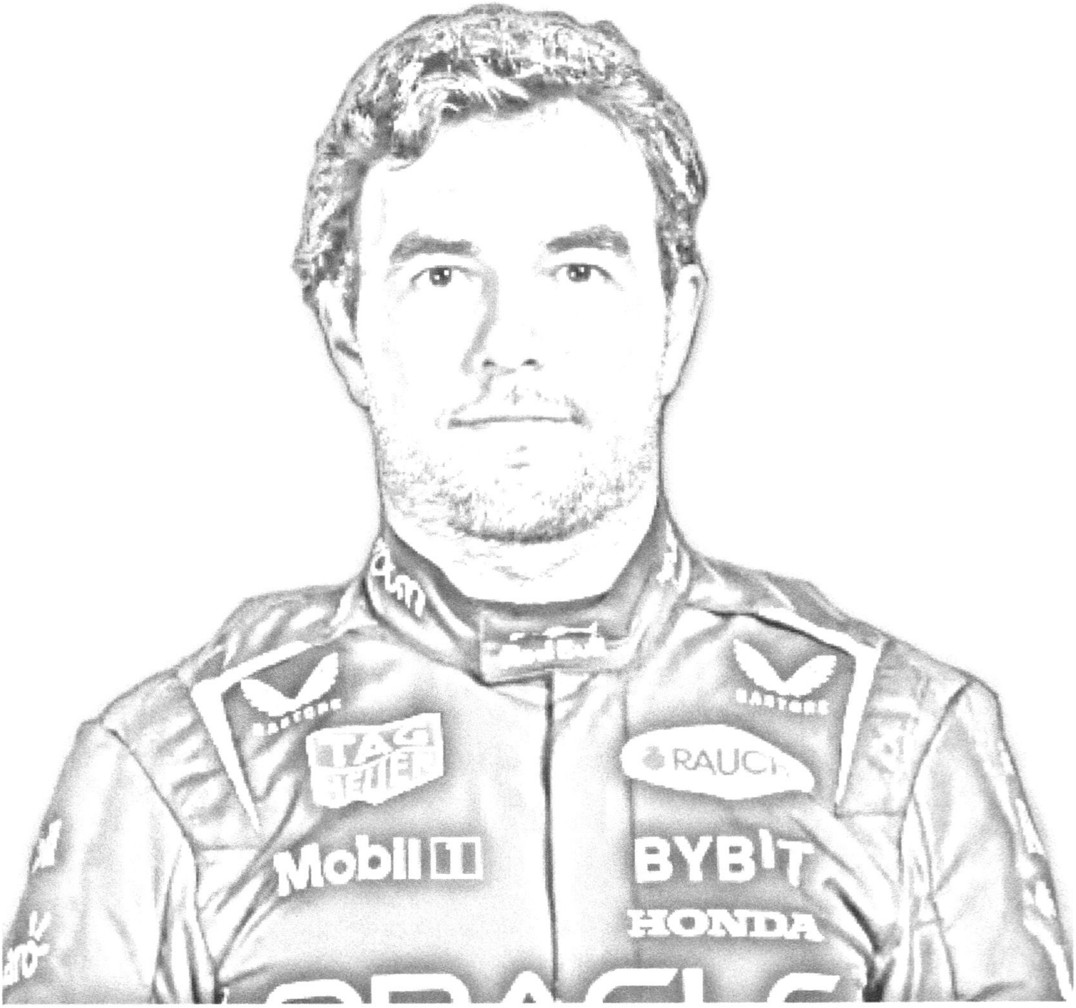

Birthday 26 January 1990
Nationality Mexican
Race number 11

First race Australia 2011
Drivers' titles 0
Podiums 35

Gin And Tequila Pineapple Punch

Checo loves his tequila, and this cocktail is boozy, zesty, and fruity – perfect for hot days and post-race refreshers and all-night parties.

45 ml gin
45 ml pineapple juice
10 ml Cointreau
10 ml lime juice
5 ml tequila

Add all the ingredients to a shaker with ice and shake well. Strain into a rocks glass with ice and garnish with fresh pineapple and a sprig of mint.

Recommended: New Harbour Distillery Rooibos Gin.

Pierre Gasly

Birthday 7 February 1996
Nationality French
Race number 10

First race Malaysia 2017
Drivers' titles 0
Podiums 4

French 75

This bubbly tipple is, like Pierre, stylish, sophisticated, and delicious. I mean, uhm. French**.

I can verify the cocktail is delicious from first-hand experience.

As for Pierre, one needs to rely on one's eyes and active imagination. Best contemplated with a drink in hand.

15 ml lemon juice
15 ml simple syrup
60 ml gin
MCC, champagne, or prosecco, chilled

Add the lemon juice, simple syrup, and to a shaker with ice and shake until well-chilled.

Strain into a champagne flute and fill slowly with the bubbly of your choice.
Garnish with a lemon twist.

Recommended: Mirari Celebration Gin.

** French 75 may be from New York or Paris. Who knows for sure?

Champagne, Prosecco, and MCC

"Bubbly" can only be termed Champagne if it is produced in the Champagne region of France. It is fermented twice, with the secondary fermentation taking place in the bottle with the addition of yeast and solids that provide the bubbles.

Prosecco is a sparkling wine produced primarily in the Veneto region of Italy, made using the Charmat process, comprising a single fermentation in a tank followed by a pressured bottling.

South African MCC (Méthode Cap Classique) offers tiny, wonderfully effervescent bubbles and closely resembles the champagne process.

George Russell

Birthday 15 February 1998
Nationality British
Race number 63

First race Australia 2019
Drivers' titles 0
Podiums 11

Earl Grey Marteani

Earl Grey tea and George Russell are as British as it gets. Egg whites make this cocktail smoother – like George's chest – and richer – like his accent – softening the bite of the gin and tea. Aquafaba is a popular vegan alternative to egg whites that yields a similar texture and flavour.

40 ml Earl-Grey tea-infused gin***
20 ml lemon juice
30 ml simple syrup
1 egg white

Half-rim a couple glass with sugar and set aside.
Add the ingredients to a shaker without ice and dry-shake vigorously for at least ten seconds.

Add ice and shake until well-chilled.
Strain into the coupe glass and garnish with a lemon twist.

Recommended: Hope Navy Strength Gin.

*** Add 65 ml of Earl Grey tea leaves to a 750 ml bottle of navy strength gin.
Seal, shake, and let it sit at room temperature for two to eight hours.
Strain the gin though a coffee filter into another container.

Rinse out remaining tea leaves in the gin bottle and pour the infused gin back into the bottle.

Refrigerate indefinitely.

What is Navy Strength Gin?

Any gin with more than 57.15% alcohol is considered to be navy strength. Generally, gin has 43% alcohol.

The high alcohol concentration was practical at sea. Below deck, gin and rum were stored in wooden barrels alongside explosives. The alcohol percentage had to be at least 57.15% in case it started leaking and soaking into the gunpowder. Anything less, and the gunpowder will not burn.

The "proof" test used by the British Royal Navy entailed sprinkling gin on gunpowder. If the powder burned after being soaked, it was "gunpowder proof" and the gin was allowed on board.

Alex Albon

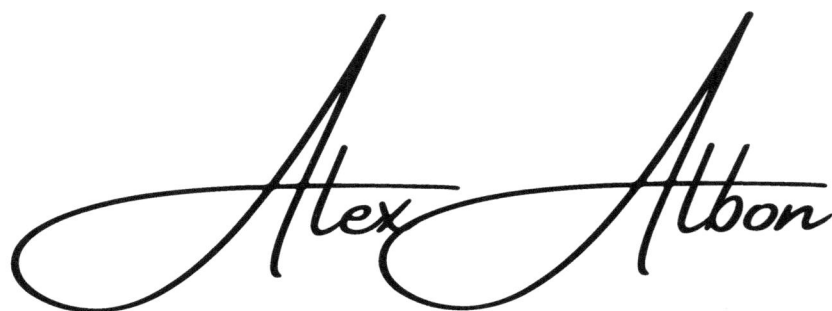

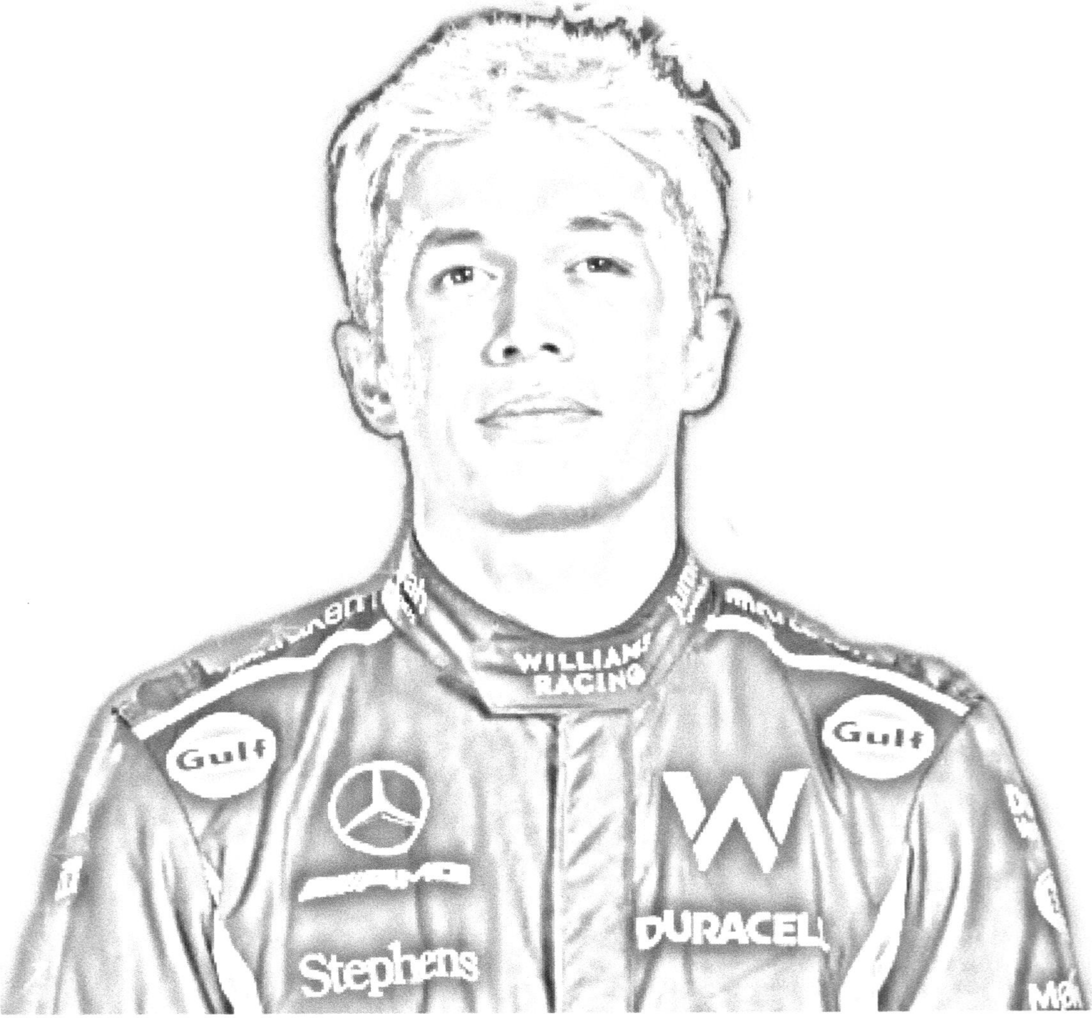

Birthday 23 March 1996
Nationality Thai
Race number 23

First race Australia 2019
Drivers' titles 0
Podiums 2

Bangkok G&T

Like Alex, this cocktail is light and refreshing. The Thai-British driver doesn't take himself too seriously, is the perfect Insta-boyfriend for his girlfriend, and has a whole menagerie of cats, a dog, and a horse with their dedicated Instagram page.

20 (Thai) basil leaves
60 ml gin
30 ml lemon juice
30 ml simple syrup
250 ml tonic water

Add the basil leaves, gin, lemon juice, and simple syrup to a cocktail shaker and break up the leaves with a muddler.

Then strain the liquid into an ice-filled highball glass and top up with tonic water. Give it a gentle stir and garnish with a basil leaf and lemon slice.

Recommended: Gin Mare Mediterranean Gin*.

Thai Basil vs Sweet Basil

Thai basil has a purple stem, while sweet basil has a green stem. And, unlike sweet basil's delicate, floppy leaves, Thai basil leaves are considerably tougher, which means they'll hold up better throughout cooking. Sweet basil leaves are usually added fresh, after the rest of the meal has been cooked.

Sweet basil has a milder peppery and sweet flavour than Thai basil, which has a spicy, anise or liquorice-like flavour.

If you can't find Thai basil, you can use sweet basil. The most important consideration is that you use the highest-quality ingredients you can afford.

Oscar Piastri

Birthday 6 April 2001
Nationality Australian
Race number 81

First race Bahrain 2023
Drivers' titles 0
Podiums 2

New Fashioned

As the newer Aussie on the grid I thought this would be a good choice. And does the guy have personality!

His dry sense of humour and perpetual chill makes him a favourite of the media and among the drivers. And if you don't follow his mom on social media, you're missing out!

60 ml gin
5 ml simple syrup
A dash of Angostura bitters
A dash of orange bitters

Place a large piece of ice in a tumbler.
Add the gin and syrup, splash on the bitters, and garnish with lime peel.

This should be enjoyed slowly, letting the flavours evolve as the ice melts.

Just like Oscar's jokes and expresions.

Recommended: Cruxland Gin.

That Tweet

As the driver in the tug-of-war between McLaren and Alpine over his services for 2023, Oscar Piastri chose to leave Alpine after a breakdown in trust with the team.

The young Australian driver claimed there was a lack of clarity around his future at Alpine. He said he twice told Alpine he would be leaving the team well in advance of Fernando Alonso's departure, which led to the team "falsely" announcing him as a 2023 driver. In response, Piastri tweeted:

"I understand that, without my agreement, Alpine F1 have put out a press release late this afternoon that I am driving for them next year. This is wrong and I have not signed a contract with Alpine for 2023. I will not be driving for Alpine next year."

Yuki Tsunoda

Birthday 11 May 2000
Nationality Japanese
Race number 22

First race Bahrain 2021
Drivers' titles 0
Podiums 0

Neighbourhood Negroni

During the 2023 season, Yuki mentioned in a media interview that when he scores points, he's allowed a Negroni. Not the drink I'd have thought of, but it's wonderful to learn more about the drivers, their habits, and their favourites.

30 ml gin
30 ml Campari
30 ml sweet vermouth

Add all the ingredients to an ice-filled mixing glass and stir until well-chilled.
Strain into a chilled rocks glass.
Ice is optional, as is the orange wheel garnish.

Recommended: Ugly Gin.

Zhou Guanyu

Birthday 30 May 1999
Nationality Chinese
Race number 24

First race Bahrain 2022
Drivers' titles 0
Podiums 0

Gin and Earl Grey Bubble Tea

Zhou's love for bubble tea is well-known. His helmet design for the Singapore race prominently featured images of the refreshing beverage. Like the Chinese driver, this cocktail is unassuming but sweet.

1 earl grey teabag
45 ml gin
120 ml boiled water
240 ml cold water
30 ml honey or sweetener of choice
1 tablespoon boba of choice

Steep the earl grey tea in the boiled water for four minutes.
Remove the teabag and add your sweetener, stirring until it's dissolved, and allow to cool.

Add the boba to a highball glass half-filled with ice.

Pour in the cooled tea and add the gin.

Fill up with cold water, leaving room for milk or cream if desired.

Top up with milk/cream and serve with a wide straw.

Recommended: Rhino Beetle Honey Gin.

Clear, Cracked, and Crushed Ice

To make clear ice cubes at home, boil the water to remove the small impurities that cause small imperfections in the ice.
Boil the water and let it cool. Repeat this process and cover the filled ice cube tray with plastic wrap to prevent air from getting into the water. Freeze for at least two hours.

To make cracked ice, wrap ice cubes in a clean tea towel and give it a good couple of bashes with a rolling pin.

Making crushed ice is best done with an ice crusher, blender, or food processor.

Remember that the smaller the ice particles, the faster your drink will dilute.

Daniel Ricciardo

Birthday 6 April 2001
Nationality Australian
Race number 81

First race Bahrain 2023
Drivers' titles 0
Podiums 32

Timberpoint Cooler

After Abu Dhabi 2022, many thought the charismatic Australian driver's racing days were done. But he came back halfway during 2023 full of energy and a range of questionable facial hair.

Danny Ric is every marketer's dream, but he's not everybody's cup of tea. I feel the same way about Aperol - hugely popular but maybe a bit overrated.

60 ml gin
30 ml Aperol
7 ml lime juice
15 ml simple syrup
Soda water

Add everything except the soda water in an ice-filled shaker and shake until chilled.
Strain into a chilled Collins glass half-filled with ice.
Top up with soda water and stir gently.
Garnish with a cucumber spiral.

Recommended: Muti Gin.

Chilling Glasses

Chilling glasses is best achieved in the freezer. They only need five to ten minutes.

Alternatively, fill your glass with ice before you mix your drink. Crushed ice is preferable since it makes more contact with the glass.

If you're using ice cubes, add some water to help them cool faster.

When you're ready to pour your drink, discard the ice.

Fernando Alonso

Birthday 29 July 1981
Nationality Spanish
Race number 14

First race Australia 2001
Drivers' titles 2
Podiums 106

Dirty Martini

It's a classic, like Nando. And the wily old fox has been known to have a few dirty tricks up his sleeve. As the oldest driver on the grid and showing no signs of slowing down, it's only fitting to raise a toast in one of the best ways to enjoy gin.

60 ml gin
30 ml dry vermouth
A splash of olive brine

Shake the gin and vermouth over ice until well-chilled, then strain into a martini glass. Spoon in brine to taste, and garnish with three olives.

Recommended: Cape Saint Blaze Oceanic Gin.

Nico Hülkenberg

Birthday 19 August 1987
Nationality German
Race number 27

First race Bahrain 2010
Drivers' titles 0
Podiums 0

Corpse Reviver No. 2

The Super Sub is doing his second season in a full-time seat at Haas, alongside his frenemy K-Mag, who eloquently invited the German to "suck my balls, honey" following a racing incident. The Hülk is one of the most successful drivers never to have scored a podium. But he knows how to get the points.

Absinthe to rinse
20 ml gin
20 ml Lillet blanc
20 ml orange liqueur
20 ml lemon juice

Use the absinthe to rinse the inside of a chilled coupe glass and discard the excess.

Pour the rest of the ingredients in an ice-filled shaker and shake until well-iced. Strain into the prepared glass, garnish with a maraschino cherry and serve immediately.

Recommended: Inverroche Amber Gin.

Choosing a Garnish

There are three approaches for deciding which garnish to combine with your gin: complement, contrast, and harmonise.

Making your drink more complex makes it more interesting.

For a complementary garnish, find something that brings out the flavours of your gin.

Choose a garnish that adds depth if you wish to contrast it.

Finally, a harmonising garnish highlights the gin's dominant flavour while adding complexity.

Valtteri Bottas

Birthday 28 August 1989
Nationality Finnish
Race number 77

First race Australia 2013
Drivers' titles 0
Podiums 67

Naked Peach

On 11 May 2022 VB posted a pic of his bare behind soaking in a stream in Aspen, Colorado. It was uncaptioned, but naturally, it went viral moments after being published. And so, when I stumbled across this recipe, I knew exactly where to slot it into my collection.

The Fin has also launched his 2024 Bottass Calendar in November, pledging a portion of the proceeds to prostate cancer research.

He also shaved his famous moustache at the start of Movember and shared the progress of his regrowth to continuously raise awareness of the cause.

One large ripe or roasted peach (cut the peach in half, remove the stone, roast until soft).

1 teaspoon light brown sugar
15 ml lime juice
60 ml gin
A pinch of lime zest
15 ml rosemary syrup
Chilled lemonade

Purée the peach, sugar, and lime juice in a blender and strain through a fine sieve.
Shake the gin, stained peach purée, lime zest and syrup over ice.
Pour into a coupe glass and top with lemonade.
Garnish with a sprig of rosemary and fresh peach slices.

Recommended: Jorgensen's Pepper Gin.

Disclaimer I: Ideally Valtteri's cocktail would've featured Oath gin but seeing as how I can't get my hands on some, I had to improvise.

Disclaimer II: I was going to give the espresso martini to VB but this cocktail's name had Valtteri written all over it.

Carlos Sainz Jr

Birthday 1 September 1994
Nationality Spanish
Race number 55

First race Australia 2015
Drivers' titles 0
Podiums 18

Qui-Gon-Gin-Singer

I don't know if the Smooth Operator is a Star Wars fan, but he does love his coffee. I didn't want to throw in an espresso martini, and "Coffee & Cigarettes" didn't seem suitable either.

In 2022 it seemed like if a track had a gravel trap, the sporty Spaniard would take his Ferrari F1-75 rallying.

This resulted in several memes, since Carlos Sainz Sr. is a World Rally Champion. So more than petrol, gravel seems to be the familial passion.

Mix up this drink – as tall, cool, and handsome as this half of Carlando.

60 ml gin
180 ml cold-brew coffee
60 ml tonic water

Pour the tonic into a highball glass filled with ice.
Combine the gin and coffee in a mixing glass, give it a stir, and pour it over the tonic.
Express a lemon twist's oil over the glass and use it as garnish.

Recommended: Lieben Sailor Gin.

Coffee and Gin

Coffee is a popular beverage. When its complex flavours are blended with gin, the result is a really effective crossover.

The rich fragrance of coffee adds a beautiful, smokey aroma to any cocktail to which it is added. It's why coffee cocktails are eternal classics and coffee-centric beverages remain a focus of experimentation.

When you combine a fine gin with coffee, you get a succession of nuances, scents, and flavours that are so distinct that they accentuate the genuine flavour of the coffee and the gin.

Esteban Ocon

Birthday 17 September 1996
Nationality French
Race number 31

First race Belgium 2016
Drivers' titles 0
Podiums 3

Gin Gimlet

This drink is strong and simple, like Esteban's determination to have a successful F1 career. There's been highs and lows, and he seems quite happy at Alpine at the moment.

30 ml lime cordial (Rose's does a good job)
60 ml gin

Gently stir with ice in a shaker. You don't want chips of ice to break off and dilute your drink.
Strain into a chilled martini glass. Garnish with a slice of lime.

Recommended: Belladonna Nightshade Gin to make it Alpine pink.

Max Verstappen

Birthday 30 September 1997
Nationality Dutch
Race number 1

First race Australia 2015
Drivers' titles 3
Podiums 98

Classic G&T

Max has often mentioned his preference for a few gins and tonics. The recipe is dead simple too. The ideal ratio for a perfect G&T is one part gin to four parts of tonic water served with four blocks of ice in a highball glass.

50 ml gin
200 ml tonic
Ice

Build in the glass and garnish with a lemon slice, or whatever strikes your fancy.

Recommended: Triple Three Just Juniper Berry Gin.

Kevin Magnussen

Birthday 5 October 1992
Nationality Danish
Race number 20

First race Australia 2014
Drivers' titles 0
Podiums 1

Great Dane

When K-Mag returned to the sport in 2022 after Haas called him up to replace Nikita Mazepin, the Dane jumped into the new spec car and started earning points.

Unfortunately, he's also known for his aggressive approach to the first corner, often getting tangled with other drivers, and bringing out the red-and-black "meatball" flag to return to the pits to have the dangerous parts replaced.

Anyhoo. Back to cocktails.

60 ml gin
30 ml cherry brandy
15 ml dry vermouth
5 ml kirsch

Shake everything over ice as vigorously as K-Mag gets off the line.
Strain into a chilled rocks glass and garnish with lemon peel and cherries.

Recommended: Die Soet Rooinek Cherry Gin.

Haas – Last Chance Saloon?

Both Nico Hülkenberg and K-Mag are veteran F1 drivers called to duty for the American Haas team.

Understandably, after a lot of time and money wasted by rookie drivers catapulting into walls, the team decided to go with experience from 2023. However, the team dropped from their eight-position finish in the 2022 season to dead last in 2023.

There are some observers who feel that Andretti's bid to join the grid - if not as an eleventh team - should be to replace Haas as an authentically American team with a passion for achievement to match.

Charles Leclerc

Birthday 16 October 1997
Nationality Monagasque
Race number 16

First race Australia 2018
Drivers' titles 0
Podiums 30

Bee's Knees

Completely biased, I think this young driver is, in fact, the bee's knees and I've all my bits crossed that he wins the championship in 2024. This drink is as sweet as this man's smile.

OK. The recipe.

30 ml gin
10 ml lemon juice
20 ml clear honey
Dry lemon (also called bitter lemon in some places)

Add the gin, lemon juice, and honey to an ice-filled shaker and shake it like a Polaroid picture until it's well-chilled.

Strain into a highball glass half-filled with ice and top up with the dry lemon.
Dress with lemon ribbons like you're styling the 2022 Ferrari fashion show that featured the yellow overalls.

Enjoy while scrolling through Charles' Instagram (fortunately you have a drink for any potential thirst traps).

Recommended: Six Dogs Honey Lime Gin.

Bathtub Gin

The "Bee's Knees" is a light, prohibition-era favourite claimed to be capable of masking the taste of bathtub gins.

The name "bathtub" relates to the process of manufacturing cold-compounded gin rather than how it tastes. Compounding extracts flavour compounds from botanicals into a mixture of alcohol and water. It was employed to conceal the flavour of some horrible bootlegged spirits during the prohibition era in the United States.

It may result in "louching" or clouding of the gin. This is due to a higher concentration of essential oils and associated flavour.

Lance Stroll

Birthday 29 October 1998
Nationality Canadian
Race number 18

First race Australia 2017
Drivers' titles 0
Podiums 3

Vesper

Lance is very private. 2023 was his seventh season as an F1 driver and other than that, there's not much I can't add that hasn't been said before. But he drives for Aston Martin, the car favoured by James Bond. And so, the cocktail favoured by the dashing spy.

90 ml gin
30 ml vodka
15 ml Lillet blanc

Stir all the ingredients in a mixing glass filled with ice until thoroughly chilled.
Strain into a chilled martini glass.
Express the oils from lemon peel twist, rub it along the rim of the glass, and drop the twist into the drink.

Recommended: Poetic Licence Northern Dry Gin.

Bond orders it "shaken, not stirred" but that could lead to diluting the drink. However, I don't know your life. You do you.

There are as many types of martinis as bond girls.

But what's the difference between a martini and a vesper? First, the latter is made with both gin and vodka. It's also one of the few cocktails with a definitive origin, created by Ian Fleming in his book in 1953, named after Vesper Lynd, a fictitious double agent and James Bond's love interest.

Second, because Lillet is used instead of vermouth, a Vesper is slightly bitterer than a standard Martini. The vodka also reduces the strength of the botanical aromas in the gin, making the drink less herbaceous.

Lando Norris

Birthday 13 November 1999
Nationality British
Race number 4

First race Australia 2019
Drivers' titles 0
Podiums 13

Gin and Juice – Lando's Version

Lando does not like alcohol. Or so he says. He's claimed that his perfect drink after a race is apple juice. So, this mocktail is designed with that in mind.

50 ml alcohol-free gin
200 ml clear apple juice
Ice

Build the drink in a highball glass and garnish with a sprig of mint or rosemary. Or both – I'm not here to tell you how to live your life.

Recommended: Seedlip Garden 108*.

Logan Sargeant

Birthday 31 December 2000
Nationality American
Race number 2

First race Bahrain 2023
Drivers' titles 0
Podiums 0

Palm Beach

The first American F1 driver since 2015, the young driver from Florida scored a single point in the 2023 season. He's got a sweet face though, matching this sweet drink.

30 ml gin
30 ml white rum
30 ml pineapple juice

Add everything to a cocktail shaker filled with ice and shake vigorously until well-chilled.
Strain into a chilled rocks glass and serve immediately.

Recommended: Ginologist Summer Cup.

Testing, testing

February is new car reveal and testing month, with two sessions leading up to the first race in Bahrain. The first session is usually in Barcelona, with the second one in Bahrain.

If you're not sure gin is for you, and you'd like to test something gin-adjacent, meet the Pimm's Cup. Initially it was considered a health drink in the 1840s and is exceedingly refreshing on hot February sunny South African days.

It's built around the gin-based digestif liqueur, Pimm's No. 1.

60 ml Pimm's No. 1
15 ml lemon juice
Ginger ale
Cucumber slices, mint sprigs, strawberry slices

Build the drink by adding the Pimm's No. 1 and lemon juice in a highball glass over ice.
Top up with ginger ale and give it a gentle stir to combine.
Garnish with the cucumber, mint, and strawberries.
Feel free to add oranges if you can find them in season.

Closed circuit
Lap distance 5.412 km
Number of laps 57
Turns 15
DRS zones 3

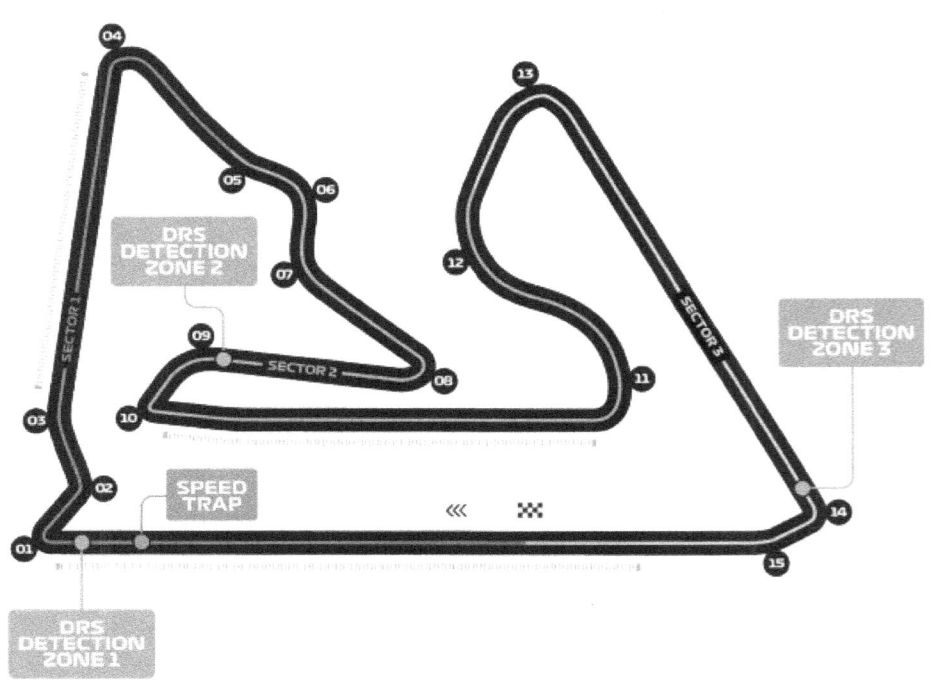

The lack of temperature and humidity in Bahrain have a significant impact on the cars. The track features several tricky corners and hairpins, and the elevation changes as the lap progresses.

The Bahrain International Circuit is a typical Hermann Tilke layout, with long straights and slow corners. The cars travel in a clockwise direction, like most circuits.

Since 2014, the race has been run after sunset with floodlights illuminating the track for television and drivers.

 The drivers first lined up for the Bahrain Grand Prix in 2004 under an unusually cloudy sky. The circuit generally offers great racing and plenty of overtaking.

However, the drivers must compete against wind, racing under floodlights, and the challenge of finding a good set-up due to the wide temperature fluctuations between sessions.

Firefly

30 ml gin
15 ml tequila
15 ml orange curaçao
15 ml lemon juice
Egg white/aquafaba

Shake all the ingredients over ice until well-chilled.
Strain into a chilled coupe glass and decorate with an orange peel twist.
Serve immediately.

Recommended: Boplaas 8 Citrus Gin.

Aquafaba

Although egg white is a traditional cocktail ingredient, many are put off by the concept of using it in their beverages. Cocktails containing egg whites are also off-limits for vegans and those with egg allergies.

That's why, in place of egg white, numerous mixologists have been using aquafaba — the liquid from cooked beans (specifically chickpeas or garbanzo beans) — in cocktails. The chickpea brine's plant starches and proteins can be whisked or shaken to generate a frothy, foamy texture.

Aquafaba began as a baking alternative for egg white. It produces a wonderful frothiness in cocktails and has no discernible flavour.

Street circuit

Lap distance 6.175 km

Number of laps 50

Turns 27

DRS zones 3

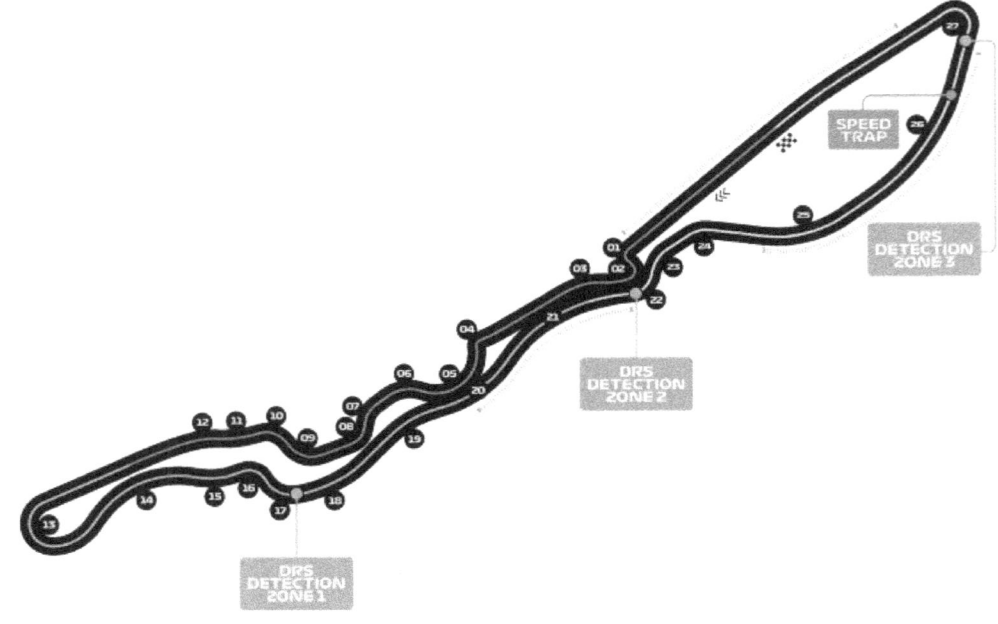

Despite featuring a few permanent sections, the Jeddah Corniche Circuit is a temporary street circuit located on a 30-kilometre coastal resort area in the ancient city of Jeddah.

The track was designed by the Tilke company and Formula 1's own Motorsports team. Following an early consideration of potential layouts using Google Earth, the track delivers fast sweeping corners that challenge the drivers.

The first Saudi Arabian Grand Prix took place under the lights in 2021. It holds the title as the fastest street circuit ever seen in Formula 1.

Ginger Rogers

38 to 10 mint leaves
20 ml ginger syrup
60 ml London dry gin
30 ml lemon juice, freshly squeezed
About 60 ml ginger ale, chilled, to top

Gently muddle the mint leaves and ginger syrup in a Collins glass
Add the gin, lemon juice, and ice.
Top with the ginger ale and stir gently.
Garnish with a mint sprig.

Recommended: Cape Town Gin Classic Dry.

London Dry Gin

London Dry Gin is one of the best gins available. Its predominant flavour is juniper berries.

London Dry Gin does not have to be produced in London; it's about how it's produced.

Although all London Dry gins are distilled, not all distilled gins are London Drys. Both are the result of double distillation. The basic alcohol must be distilled a second time with additional flavourings, the most important of which being juniper berries.

Any botanicals added after distillation prohibit the spirit from being referred to as a London Dry Gin, however it can be referred to as a distilled gin.

Street circuit
Lap distance 5.303 km
Number of laps 58
Turns 16
DRS zones 2

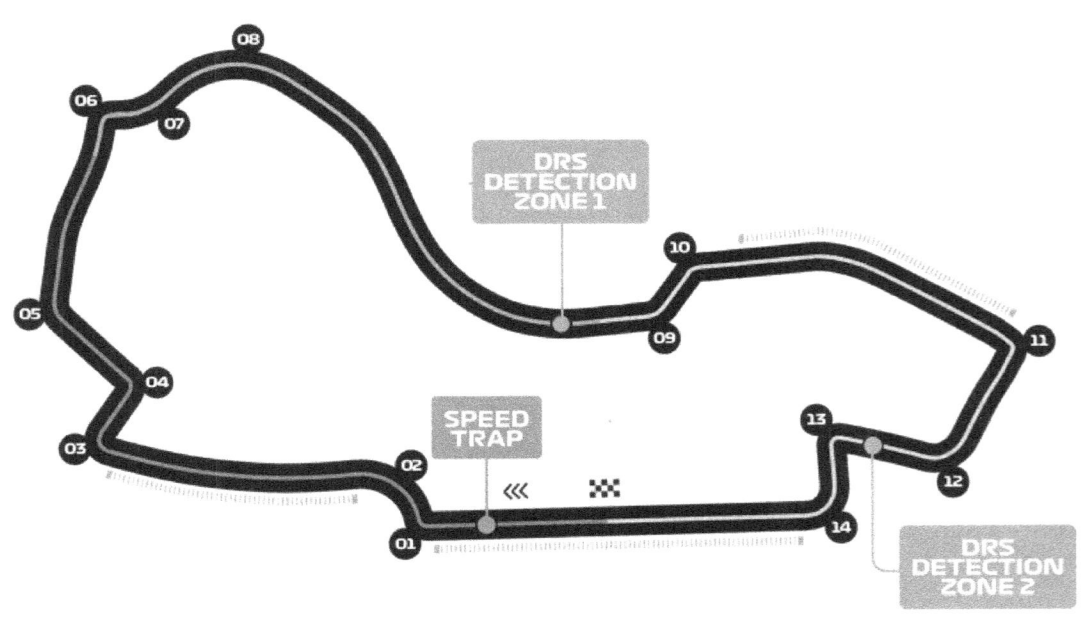

Albert Park's temporary circuit has been used since 1996, winding around the Albert Park Lake, offering picturesque low trees and high sun.

The track is filled with fast flowing turns and features a notoriously slippery surface.

Usually, the southern hemisphere enjoys early autumn days in April with some scorchers trying to hold on to summer. For these days, you need some extra chill – not only on-track.

While not quite as fast as the Jeddah track, it is one of the faster ones on the calendar.

Gin, Cherry & Apple Slushie

Serves four (4).

150 g fresh cherries with the stones removed
30 ml lemon juice
50 g light brown sugar
240 ml gin
600 ml apple juice
Lots of ice

Add the cherries, lemon juice, and sugar in a saucepan and gently heat until the sugar has dissolved, and the cherries broken down. Remove from the heat and allow to cool for five minutes.

Transfer the cooled cherry mixture to a blender and blend until smooth. You can also use a stick blender in the saucepan.

Push the blended mix through a fine sieve to make a purée.

Place the cherry purée, gin, apple juice, and ice in a blender. Blend until smooth.

Serve immediately.

Recommended: Simply based on its ingredients, I'm sure Oath gin would be ideal for this.

However, .L-Gin Lush is perfect.

Closed circuit
Lap distance 5.807 km
Number of laps 53
Turns 18
DRS zones 1

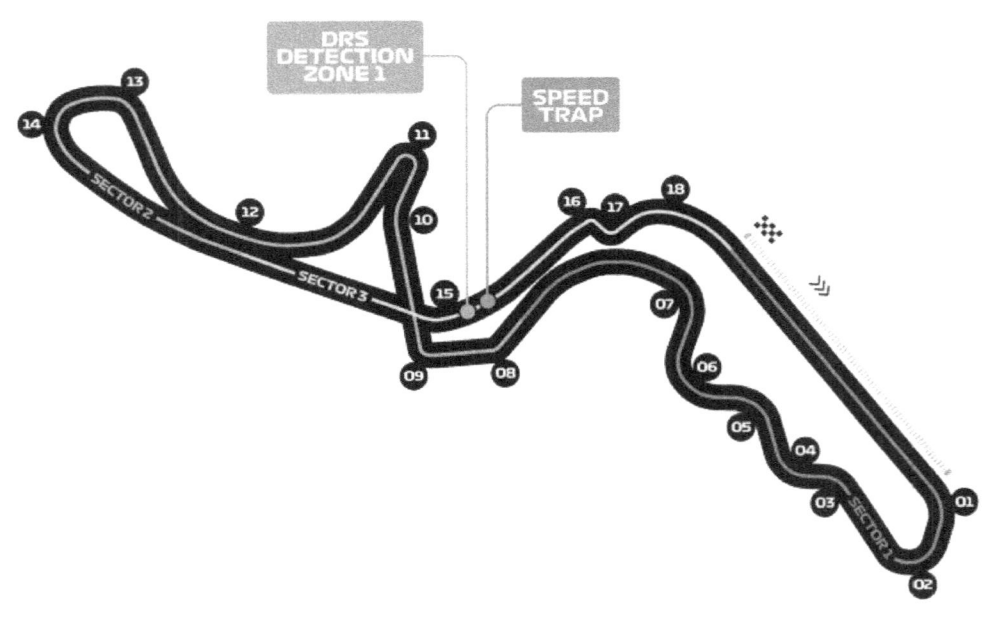

The Japanese circuit is nearly perfect in terms of track design. Suzuka has every track feature you can think of and has established itself as one of the most feared, respected, and challenging circuits on the F1 calendar since its inception in 1987.

In addition, Suzuka produces champions. Senna, Prost, Schumacher, Hill, Hakkinen, Vettel, and last year, Verstappen.

Only the best can conquer Asia's most difficult track. It takes guts, daring, and a heaping helping of talent.

If a racing driver says he doesn't love Suzuka, he's lying.

It is littered with legendary corners, each with its own backstory: the spoon curve, the Degners, the chicane, the 'S' curves, and, most notably, the iconic 130R, a corner to rival Spa's Eau Rouge.

And it is one of only a few circuits in the world with a figure-eight layout. The back straight crosses the front section, which is unusual in F1.

This cocktail is as simple as the iconic track is challenging and as potent as the track is legendary.

Saketini

90 ml gin
30 ml sake

Shake the ingredients vigorously over ice until well-chilled.
Strain into a chilled martini glass and garnish with a lemon peel twist.
Serve immediately.

Recommended: Pienaar & Son Orient Gin.

China (Shanghai)

Closed circuit
Lap distance 5.451 km
Number of laps 56
Turns 16
DRS zones 2

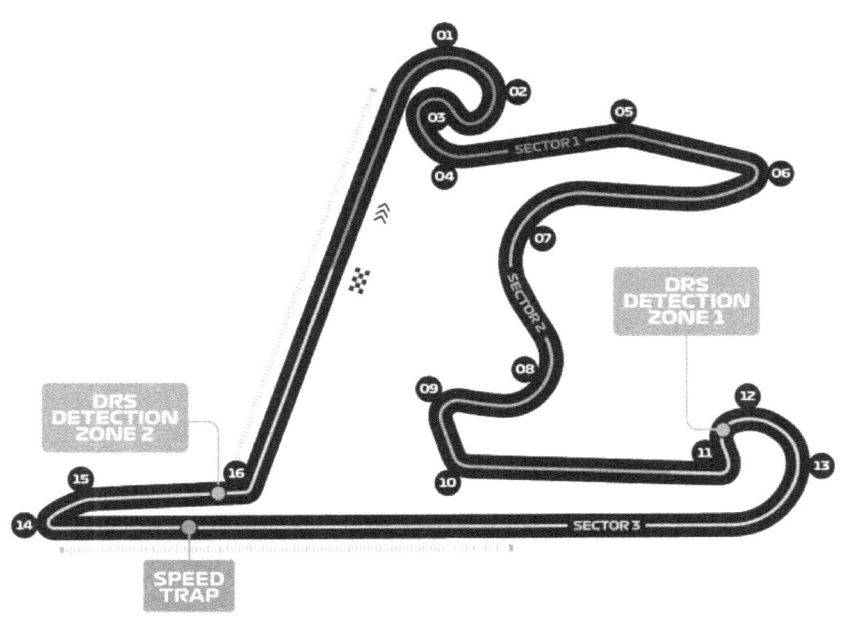

The Shanghai International Circuit is most famous for hosting the Formula 1 Chinese Grand Prix since 2004.

However, the track also hosts the annual FIA World Endurance Championship, MotoGP Chinese Grand Prix, and many national championships.

The track site was originally a swampland used as rice paddy fields, so it required extensive groundworks to construct the circuit. The enormous complex is dominated by the main grandstand and pit complex featuring wing-like viewing platforms at either end.

In addition, each F1 team had its own paddock building, arranged like pavilions in a lake.

Cucumber Matcha

Serves six (6).

7 ml Matcha green tea
500 ml water
125 ml gin
60 ml lime juice
45 ml cucumber syrup
Cucumber slices
Mint leaves

Place the matcha in a large mixing bowl and gradually add 30 ml of water, a little at a time, while constantly mixing to make a smooth matcha paste. Then gradually add the remaining water, followed by the gin, lime juice, and cucumber syrup.
Muddle some cucumber slices and mint leaves in each of the six cocktail jars.

Then, add some lime slices and ice and top up with the cucumber matcha cocktail.

Recommended: Flowstone Wild Cucumber Gin.

Miami

Street circuit
Lap distance 5.410 km
Number of laps 57
Turns 19
DRS zones 3

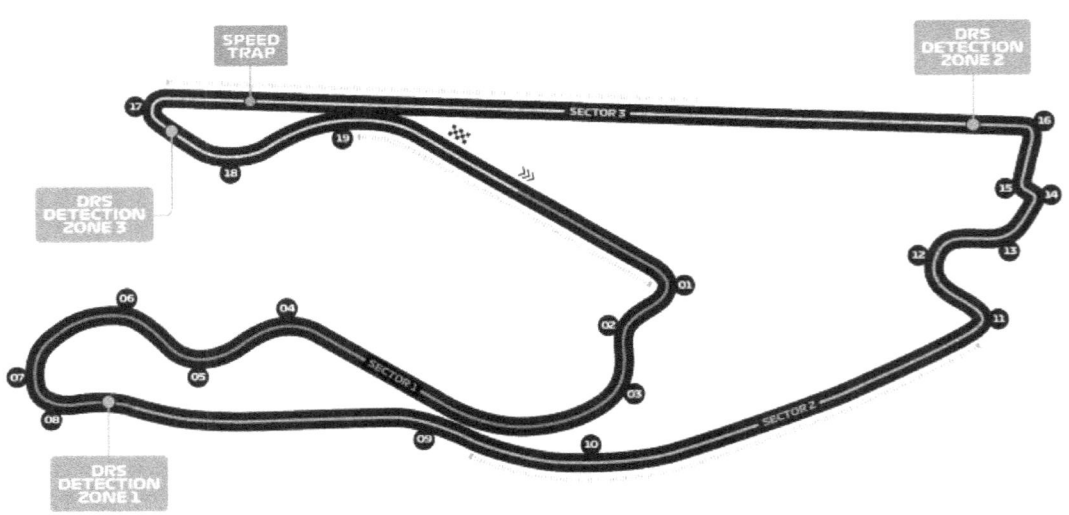

The Miami International Autodrome is a temporary F1 track that made its debut in 2022, and is set in the Hard Rock Stadium complex in Miami Gardens.

Following 36 different layout simulations, the circuit was designed with 19 thrilling turns. It was the 11th different American venue to host an F1 world championship round.

One of the greatest talking points around this track was its, erm, marina, which is as fake as… well, you can finish that yourself. A good cocktail could help you forget about it, though.

Beach House

60 ml gin
15 ml lime juice
Chilled coconut water

Pour the gin and lime juice into a highball glass filled with crushed ice.
Top up with coconut water, stir, and garnish with a lime slice.

Recommended: Blossom & Hops Gin.

According to F1 fans on social media, the Miami Grand Prix should be scrapped because the circuit is "boring." The race, staged at the Miami International Autodrome, was just added to the F1 schedule in 2022, but there are already cries from fans to have it removed permanently.

On the other hand, the much-criticised Las Vegas GP turned out to be many fans' favourite race of the season, with thrilling overtakes and close calls with the walls.

However, money talks and Liberty Media (Formula One Group) is determined to make F1 big in the US, so Miami will stick around at least for the remainder of its 10-year contract.

Italy (Imola)

Closed circuit
Lap distance 4.909 km
Number of laps 63
Turns 19
DRS zones 1

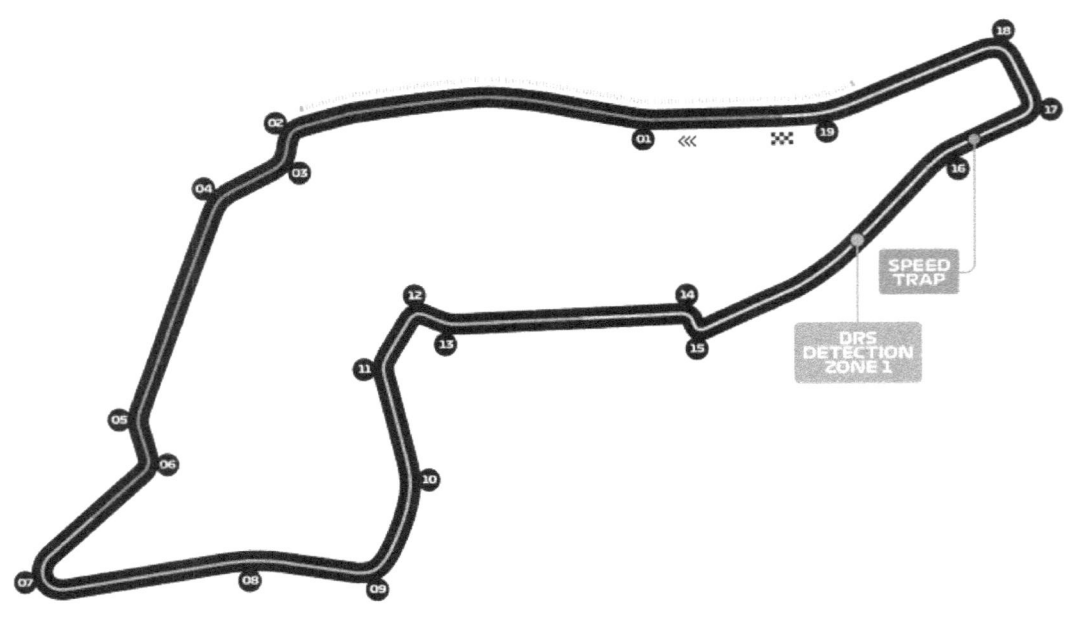

Imola hosted its first non-championship F1 race in 1963, but it took some wrangling with Monza in 1980 before the track was given the honour of hosting the Italian Grand Prix for the first time that year.

Since 1981, the two tracks have been in on the calendar. The anti-clockwise circuit is fast and has an old-school feel, with drivers putting everything on the line in iconic corners like the Acque Minerali and Piratella.

Valentino

60 ml gin
15 ml Campari
15 ml sweet vermouth

Add all the ingredients to a mixing glass filled with ice.

Stir until well-chilled then strain into a chilled cocktail glass.
Garnish with an orange twist

Recommended: Musgrave Original 11.

Imola 2023 Cancelled

In 2023, the Emilia Romagna Grand Prix was cancelled during the week in the run-up to the race when heavy storms in the area stranded residents and claimed several lives.

F1 and the FIA, in agreement with the Italian government, cancelled the race for that weekend, deciding that emergency resources would be better used elsewhere.

Several teams and drivers shared links to raise funds for humanitarian efforts, and Yuki Tsunoda was seen in the streets, helping with the clean up.

Monaco

Street circuit
Lap distance 3.337 km
Number of laps 78
Turns 19
DRS zones 1

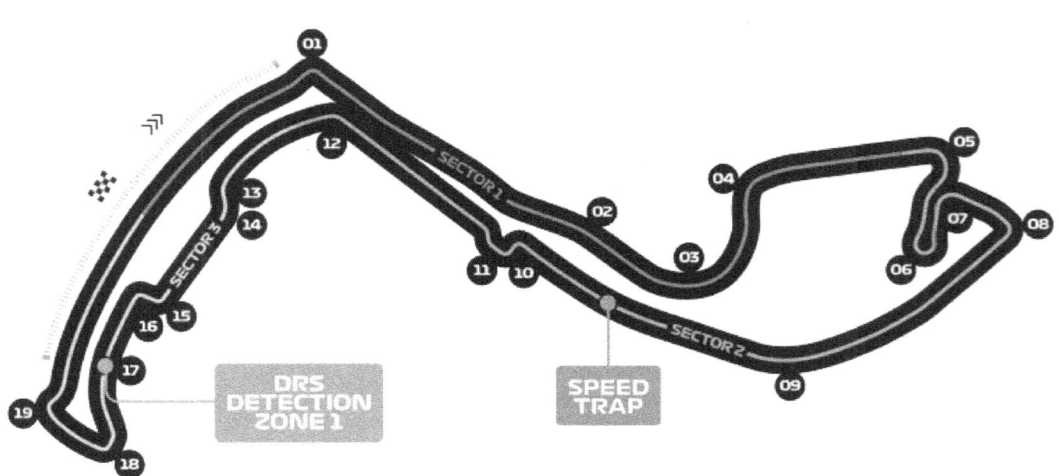

There's more to the legendary Monaco circuit than just its location and races. It possesses vast wealth, history, pedigree, and global recognition.

The race takes place in the narrow streets that run alongside the Mediterranean. The race at the end of May truly encapsulates Formula 1. Monaco is the spiritual home of Formula One, with its sun, sea, rich, beautiful people, glitz, and glamour. Since 1929, the streets of Monte-Carlo have hosted a Grand Prix. Ayrton Senna, who won the legendary GP six times, remains the greatest driver around the Monaco circuit.

The track has remained largely unchanged. Sainte Devote is still one of the most difficult first corners on the calendar, the hairpin is the slowest, and the swimming pool section is still littered with expensive yachts.

Mastering Monaco requires more than just guts. The driver must be daring to produce the perfect lap. He must position his car as close to the walls as possible, even bouncing off them on occasion.

The most important aspect of the weekend is qualifying. It is extremely rare for the man on pole to lose the race, and Saturday's session is critical to the outcome. The track is entirely made up of public roads and is famous for its lack of overtaking.

Monte Carlo

15 ml gin
7 ml lemon juice
Chilled champagne
7 ml crème de menthe

Pour the gin and lemon juice into a mixing glass half-filled with ice and stir until well-chilled.

Strain into a chilled champagne flute and top up with champagne.

Drizzle the crème de menthe over the top.

Decorate with a mint sprig and serve immediately.

Recommended: Blind Tiger Original Gin.

The Monaco/Charles Leclerc curse

The Monaco Grand Prix proudly boasts one native to represent this Principality when the series rolls into town, but while fans cheer on Charles Leclerc from the stands, the streets of Monte Carlo have never been as welcoming.

Leclerc won the Formula 2 championship in 2017, but there were no wild celebrations in Monaco that year. He had to retire from the feature race due to a suspension failure, and from the sprint race because of electrical issues.

In 2018 he joined the F1 grid for the Sauber team. However, his first F1 race in Monaco was far from memorable, with braking issues sending Leclerc into the back of Brendon Hartley's Toro Rosso on Lap 72.

Leclerc joined the Ferrari team in 2019, and the team took a gamble by not sending Leclerc out again in the first stage of qualifying, confident that the time he had on the board was sufficient. Reader, it was not.

After starting from P15, the young Monegasque was determined to show that you can overtake in Monaco. But by lap 16, Leclerc crashed into the wall at Rascasse, resulting in a right-rear tyre puncture that proved fatal to his race.

Due to the Covid-19 pandemic, the 2020 Monaco Grand Prix was cancelled, but Formula One returned in 2021, and Leclerc was back for another shot at breaking the curse.

Taking pole in his Ferrari was the ideal first step, a surprise pole given the team's lack of dominance that season. Unfortunately, his pole position was confirmed in less-than-ideal circumstances, because he crashed on his final qualifying lap, effectively ending the session for all of his competitors.

The next day he hoped to start the race, but on the lap towards the grid it was clear right away that something was wrong with his Ferrari SF21. A driveshaft failure meant Leclerc was unable to compete in the race.

In 2022 Ferrari was able to challenge for the title and Charles was determined to break the Monaco curse.

He was on pole again, but the race start was delayed by 45 minutes as the rain intensified.

However, when a track transitions from wet to dry, timing the tyre change is critical. But confusion reigned as Ferrari called Leclerc into the pits, only to reverse their decision when it was too late. As a result, Leclerc finished in P4. On the upside, at least he finished.

Charles on the So-Called Curse

In a 2022 interview with F1.com, when asked about the curse, Charles said, "I don't think about it".

"Of course, it's not been the luckiest track for me overall but it's life, it happens, it's part of motorsport and sometimes things just don't go your way."

Canada (Montreal)

Closed circuit
Lap distance 4.361 km
Number of laps 70
Turns 14
DRS zones 2

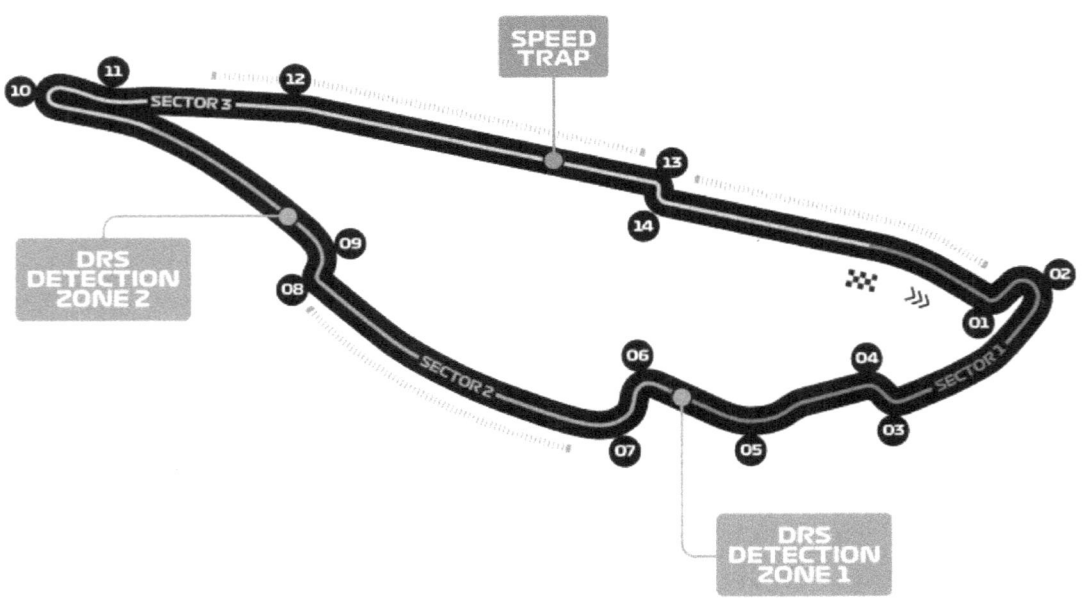

The first Canadian Grand Prix was held in 1978 on the man-made Notre Dame Island in the middle of the St Lawrence River, which was built for the 1967 Expo 67 World's Fair. Gilles Villeneuve won his first race at the track. The fast, low-downforce circuit is a favourite of the drivers.

The (in)famous Wall of Champions can be found at the Circuit Gilles Villeneuve. In qualifying, drivers accelerate through the gears to exceed 320 km/h before the braking point for turn 13 or the 'Wall of Champions.' Damon Hill, Michael Schumacher, and Jacques Villeneuve were the F1 world champions who collided with the wall in 1999, and the turn was named after them.

Jenson Button and Sebastian Vettel have since joined the list of champions, though not in a single race. The wall might have the last word. Or you could – cheers!

20 ml gin
20 ml Drambuie
20 ml maraschino liqueur
20 ml lime juice

Shake all the ingredients with ice until well-chilled.
Strain into a chilled coupe glass and garnish with a lime twist and a brandied cherry.

Recommended: Geometric Gin.

The Wall of Champions is a concrete wall at Canada's Circuit Gilles Villeneuve on the outer curve of a tight bend turning to the left of the track's last chicane, turn 13.

The wall was named when F1 world champions Damon Hill, Michael Schumacher, and Jacques Villeneuve collided with it at the 1999 Canadian Grand Prix and retired with terminal damage.

Other drivers who have crashed out into the Wall of Champions during a race include:

Ricardo Zonta (1997)
Jenson Button (2005)
Juan Pablo Montoya (2006)
Vitantonio Liuzzi (2007)
Kamui Kobayasi (2010)

Closed circuit
Lap distance 4.655 km
Number of laps 66
Turns 16
DRS zones 2

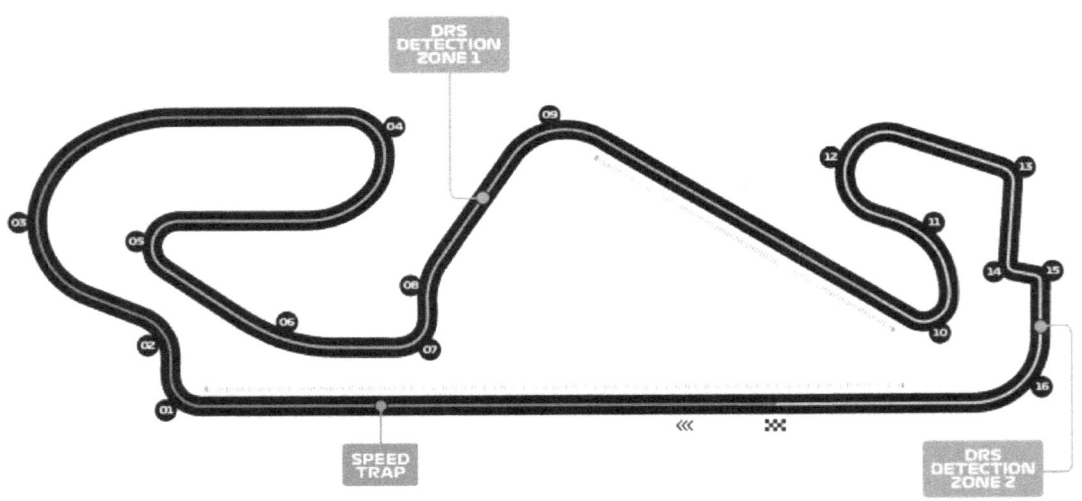

The Circuit de Barcelona-Catalunya was built as part of the 1992 Barcelona Olympics development programme and the 1991 Spanish Touring Car Championship was the first car race on the track.

Two weeks later, the track enjoyed a sensational F1 debut with Nigel Mansell and Ayrton Senna's famous drag race down the straight.

Drivers love the circuit, which also feature during winter pre-season testing. It has a good mix of high- and low-speed corners.

Agua de Valencia

Serves four to six (4 – 6).

500 ml freshly squeezed orange juice
300 ml cava/champagne/MCC
100 ml gin
100 ml vodka
Simple syrup to taste

Pour the orange juice, bubbly, gin, and vodka into a pitcher and stir gently to mix. Have a taste.
Add some simple syrup if necessary – it's not meant to be a super sweet drink, but no one wants a bitter cocktail.
Pour into chilled wine glasses with some ice and garnish with orange slices.

Recommended: Clemengold Gin.

F1 in Madrid

In December 2023, news broke about talks to take Formula 1 to the streets of Madrid from 2026.

The proposed five-kilometre parkland track would employ the IFEMA pavilion complex and fairgrounds frequently used for shows and conferences as its start-finish straight and paddock complex.

It would also use existing streets, including the M-11 highway, to loop beside Real Madrid's Valdebebas training centre and via the former Mad Cool music festival grounds.

However, with European F1 calendar spaces restricted, Madrid's impending approval will put additional pressure on Barcelona's long-term prospects.

Closed circuit
Lap distance 4.318 km
Number of laps 71
Turns 10
DRS zones 2

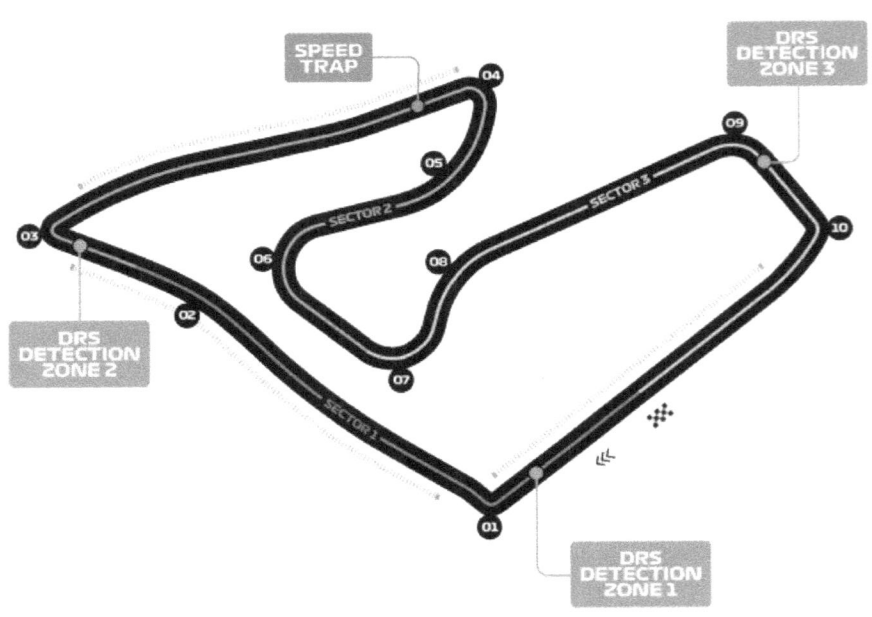

The Red Bull ring is a fairly straightforward and short track. With multiple straights supported by DRS zones and high-speed corners, a race at the Red Bull Ring almost always gives fans a good showing.

Austria, an old school circuit that once had the same levels of fear as Spa, deserves it place on the grid.

The circuit, in the south-east of the country in the beautiful Styrian Mountains in Spielberg, offers long straights, plenty of overtaking opportunities, and a rugged edge that will catch out many drivers.

Colt 45

30 ml gin
60 ml Jägermeister
120 – 180 ml Red Bull originalraph gin.

30 ml gin
60 ml Jägermeister
120 – 180 ml Red Bull original

Build the drink in a highball glass over ice and finish it off with enough Red Bull to top up the glass. Stir well and serve immediately. No need to bother with garnishes.

Recommended: Autograph gin.

I have many issues with this drink, not least of it the title. I've lived to the mature age I am successfully avoiding Jägermeister. I've also given up caffeine completely, so just know my commitment to the theme by making this abom(b)ination.

The Red Bull Ring

The Red Bull Ring was previously known as the A1 Ring and the Osterreichring. Over half of this area is mountain and forest in the heart of the Styrian highlands. Red Bull bought and renamed the circuit in 2004, modernising its infrastructure.

According to Christian Horner, team principal and CEO, Red Bull Racing's supremacy in Formula One in 2023 directly translated to stronger sales of its namesake energy drink.

Red Bull is the second-most popular energy drink brand globally, trailing only Monster Beverage. In 2024 Monster will be a sponsor for McLaren after a 14-year association with Mercedes F1.

United Kingdom
Silverstone

Closed circuit
Lap distance 5.891 km
Number of laps 52
Turns 18
DRS zones 2

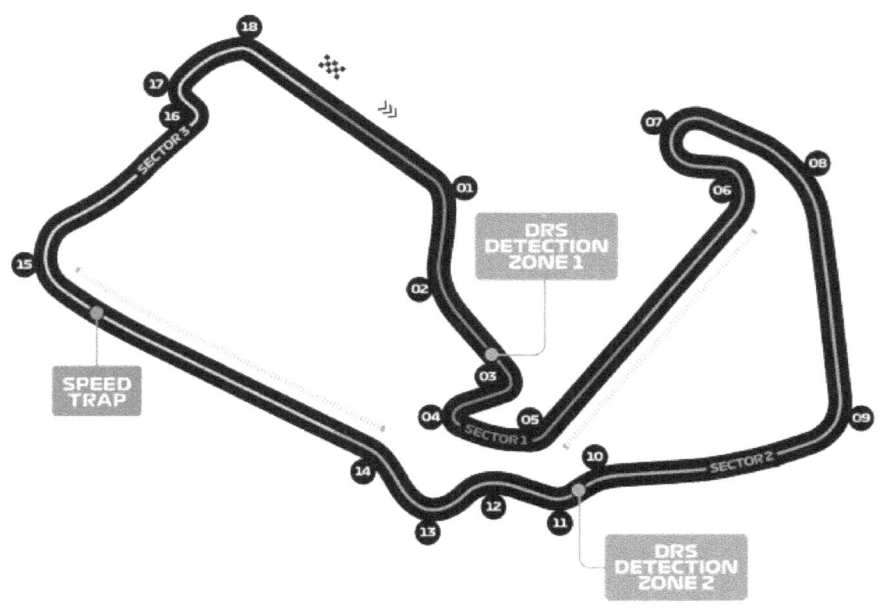

Silverstone is a perennial favourite among drivers and enthusiasts alike. It is a historic track that has been in Formula 1 since its inception, with the first championship race held there in 1950.

The perimeter road to the RAF Silverstone airfield built in 1942 was the foundation for one of the world's greatest racetracks.

Despite numerous layout changes over the years, Silverstone has always retained its essential character as one of the fastest tracks on the F1 calendar, with historic corners such as Maggotts, Becketts, and Abbey posing some of the most difficult challenges for racing drivers anywhere in the world.

Silver Fizz

5 ml white granulated sugar
15 ml lemon juice
60 ml gin
30 ml organic egg white
30 – 60 ml chilled soda water to top up

Stir the sugar and lemon juice in a shaker with a bar spoon.
Add the gin and egg white and dry shake (no ice) vigorously.
Add ice and shake again until the drink's chilled.
Strain into a chilled highball glass and top up with soda water.

Recommended: Quince Gin Classic.

Soda Water

Wondering about the difference between sparkling and soda water?

The fizz in both is created by infusing still spring water with carbon dioxide under pressure. However, soda water is further infused with bicarbonate of soda to ensure a drink retains its bubbles when alcohol is added. As a result, soda water is a little fizzier with a slightly sharper taste than sparkling water.

Fortunately, the flavour difference is so small that one can easily replace one with the other.

Both have no calories, sugar, or sweetener, making them a wonderful, safe alternative carbonated drink.

Closed circuit
Lap distance 4.381 km
Number of laps 70
Turns 14
DRS zones 1

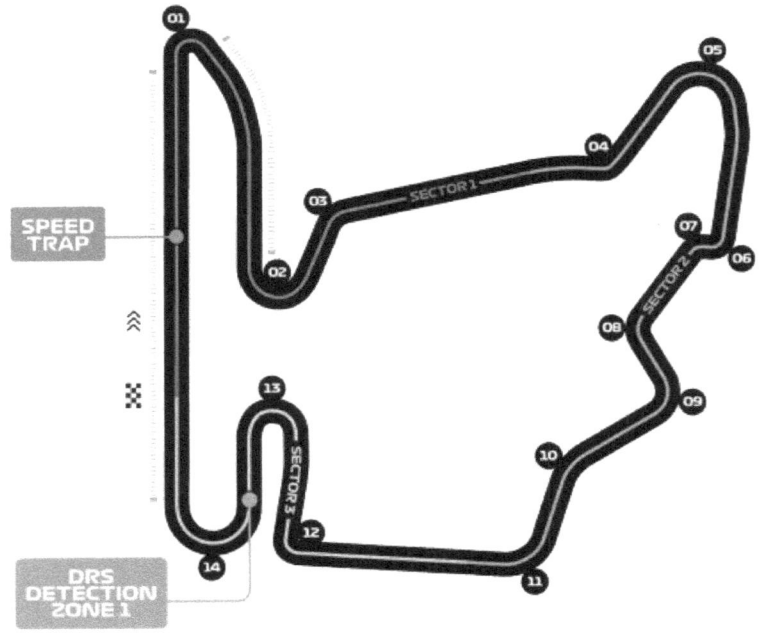

The Hungaroring hosted its first Grand Prix in 1986, when Nelson Piquet won after overtaking Ayrton Senna's on the outside to take the lead.

The circuit is often compared to a karting track because of its lack of straights.

For the race, teams opt for Monaco levels of downforce to navigate the various series of corners.

Since the track is built in a natural bowl, any of the grandstands around the main straight offers a view of other parts of the track too.

Gin-Gin Mule

One mint sprig
30 ml simple syrup
20 ml lime juice
50 ml gin
Ginger beer

Gently muddle the mint sprig, simple syrup, and lime juice in a shaker.
Add the gin and ice and shake until chilled.
Strain into a highball glass filled with ice and top up with ginger beer.
Garnish with a sprig of mint.

Recommended: D'Urban Barrel Aged Gin.

Peril on the Podium

Lando Norris is known for his signature podium celebration habit of smashing the bottom of the champagne bottle to create an impressive spray.

However, in 2023 he smashed more than just his second-place Jeroboam when the impact on the top step caused Max Verstappen's trophy to topple over and break. Lando jokingly blamed Max for placing the trophy in the way of disaster, but he did apologise.

Herend produced a replacement of the estimated $45 000 vase at no cost. This trophy was presented to Max in August, with Lando given a fake invoice and kept at arm's length.

Closed circuit
Lap distance 7.004 km
Number of laps 44
Turns 19
DRS zones 2

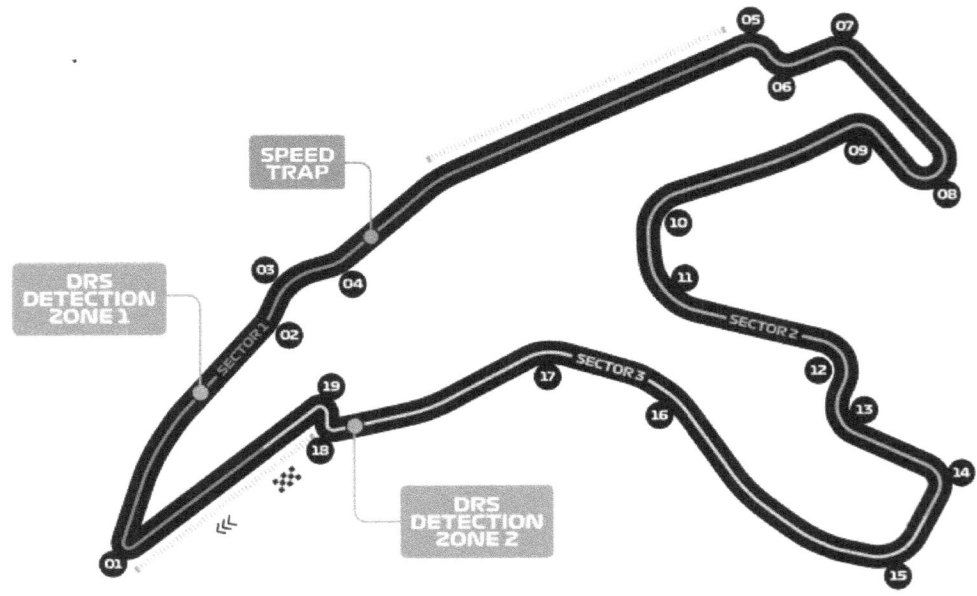

The circuit, which is frequently abbreviated as "Spa," gracefully winds through the Ardennes Forest. The original triangle-shaped track was built in 1921 using public roads between the towns of Francorchamps, Malmedy, and Stavelot to create an incredible 14.9-kilometre circuit.

The track was redeveloped in 1979, and despite being half the length of the original, it is still the longest on the current calendar at 7.004km. Because of the track's size and the nature of Belgian weather, it can sometimes rain on one section of the track while remaining dry on another, causing grip to vary from one corner to the next.

In 2019, Formula 2 racer Anthoine Hubert tragically died in an accident at the (in)famous Eau Rouge/Raidillon corner.

The young driver was a close friend of many of the current drivers, particularly Pierre Gasly and Charles Leclerc, the latter dedicating his first F1 victory to his friend that weekend.

Rosie Lee

45 ml gin
15 ml rose petal syrup
30 ml lychee juice
15 ml fresh lemon juice
1 dash Angostura bitters

Add all the ingredients to a shaker and fill with ice.
Shake, and strain into a teacup filled with fresh ice.
Garnish with a lemon wedge or orange wheel.

Recommended: Jenny Macadamia Nut Gin.

Netherlands (Zandvoort)

Closed circuit
Lap distance 4.252 km
Number of laps 72
Turns 14
DRS zones 2

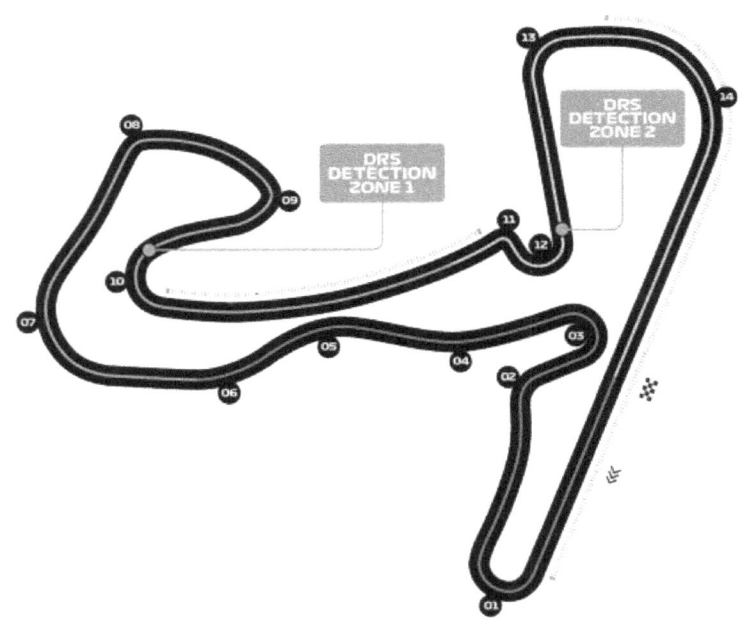

Formula 1 arrived in the Dutch dunes in 1952 and raced there on and off until 1985. In 2019, it was announced that the championship would return to Zandvoort in 2020, which was later pushed back to 2021 due to COVID-19.

The Zandvoort track swoops and flows through the sand dunes, giving the lap a rollercoaster-like feel. The circuit was modernised, including increasing the banking angle at the famous Tarzan corner to a whopping 18 degrees, resulting in a challenging drivers' track.

Gin Blossom

45 ml gin
45 ml vermouth
20 ml apricot eau de vie
2 dashes orange bitters

Add everything to a mixing glass filled with ice and stir until chilled.
Strain into a chilled coupe glass.
Garnish with an orange twist after releasing the oils from the twist over the drink.

Recommended: Monk's Mary Jane Gin.

Liam Lawson Enters the Chat

During the second practice session of the 2023 Dutch GP, Oscar Piastri and Daniel Ricciardo crashed into the barriers, the latter in an effort to avoid smashing into his countryman. Unfortunately, Daniel neglected to remove his hands from the steering wheel before the impact, resulting in a broken metacarpal bone in his left hand, leaving him unfit to continue participation.

Enter Liam Lawson, AlphaTauri's replacement driver, who during his five F1 races, finished ahead of his teammate Yuki Tsunoda twice.

Despite missing out on an F1 seat in 2024, the New Zealander's impressive debut should see him back on the grid in due time.

Italy (Monza)

Closed circuit

Lap distance 5.793 km

Number of laps 53

Turns 11

DRS zones 2

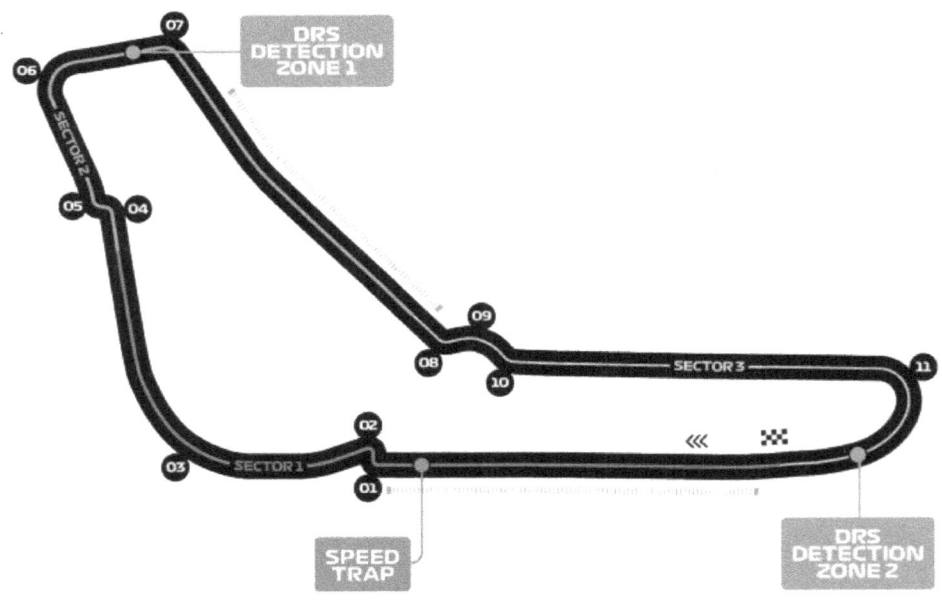

Ferrari reigns supreme among the Tifosi in Monza, with massive Prancing Horse flags and Rosso Corsa-filled stands.

The mostly straight track, as one of the quickest on the calendar, can provide an overtaking-filled Grand Prix. It was built in just 110 days and hosted its first race a week after it opened on 3 September, 1922.

The cars are on full throttle for 80% of the lap, but a series of big stops into tight chicanes puts a strain on the brakes.

Blood and Sage

Half a blood orange cut into wedges
Two fresh sage leaves
60 ml gin
20 ml lime juice
20 ml simple syrup
1 egg white

Gently muddle the orange wedges and sage leaves in a shaker.
Add the rest of the ingredients and dry shake vigorously (no ice).
Fill with ice and shake again until well-chilled.
Strain into a chilled coupe glass and garnish with a sage leaf.

Recommended: Bloedlemoen Gin.

Ten Consecutive Wins

Following the chequered flag at the 2023 Italian Grand Prix, Max Verstappen became the first-ever driver to achieve ten consecutive Grand Prix wins - one of several records he'd break during the season.

The most memorable soundbite from the race came from Mercedes F1 team boss Toto Wolff, saying, "I don't know if he cares about the records. It is not something that would be important for me, those numbers, it is for Wikipedia and nobody reads that anyway."

Other 2023 records Max gained include: most podiums in an F1 season (21); most wins in an F1 season (19); highest number of points in an F1 season (575); most expensive super licence ever (approximately €1,200,000 for 2024); longest streak of converting poles to wins (13).

Street circuit

Lap distance 6.003 km

Number of laps 51

Turns 20

DRS zones 2

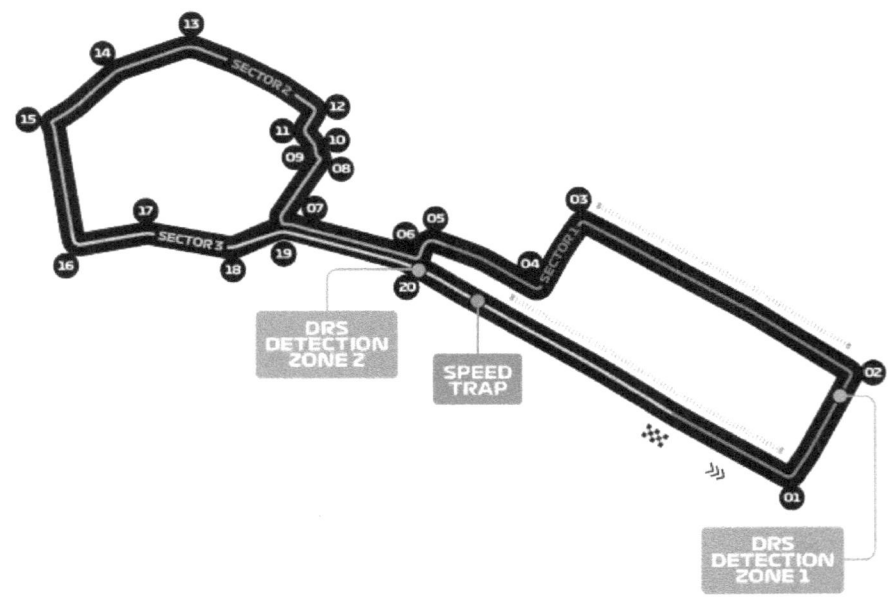

As a street track, the Baku circuit isn't exactly built, but hosted its first Formula 1 Azerbaijan Grand Prix in 2017.

The track is a mix of wide open and tight twisty turns, with a long main straight leading into turn one.

Like Monaco, the slightest mistakes can quickly turn to heartache.

When deciding on a car setup, teams must choose between downforce for the twisty bits or less drag for the straight.

Pomegranate and Mint Shrub

30 ml gin
30 ml Grand Marnier
60 ml pomegranate syrup

Build this drink in a highball glass filled with crushed ice.
Pour the ingredients into the glass and stir with a bar spoon.
Decorate with a sprig of mint and a teaspoon of pomegranate seeds.

Recommended: Black Rose Blush Gin.

Pitlane Safety Issues

During the final lap of the Azerbaijan Grand Prix, FIA-appointed personnel permitted photographers to pass into the pits' fast lane to prepare to photograph the parc fermé and podium celebrations, even though the race was still in progress.

Alpine driver Esteban Ocon still had to make a pit stop in accordance with race regulations and subsequently had to dodge multiple cameras as he approached his pit stop.

As a result, the race stewards started an investigation into the incident. They later advised that improvements be made to the end-of-race parc fermé procedures to avoid a repeat of the incident.

Street circuit

Lap distance 5.063 km

Number of laps 61

Turns 23

DRS zones 3

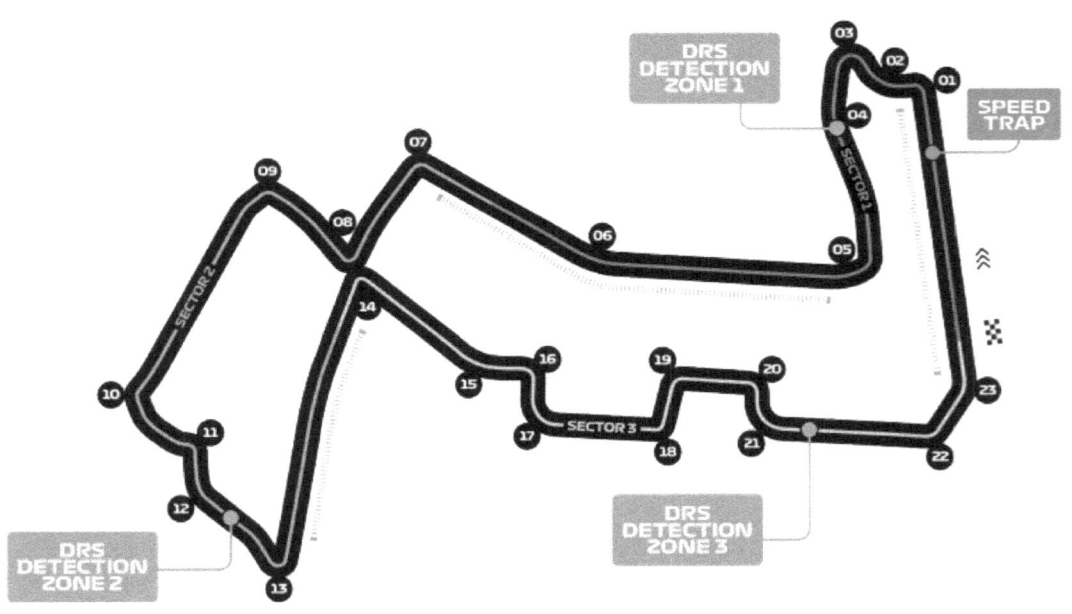

The Marina Bay Circuit debuted in 2008 to host the first night-time race in F1 history, and it quickly became a favourite among teams and drivers.

The circuit is one of the most physically demanding on the calendar, with its bumpy street surface and humid conditions keep the drivers focussed. They also work the wheel a lot around the high-speed lap.

The physical stress causing them to lose as much as 3 kg over the course of a race.

This cocktail choice is a no-brainer. Not many gin cocktails are location-specific.

Singapore Sling

60 ml gin
30 ml cherry brandy
30 ml lemon juice
5 ml grenadine
Soda water

Add the gin, cherry brandy, lemon juice, and grenadine to a cocktail share filled with ice. Shake until well-frosted.
Half-fill a chilled tall glass with cracked ice and strain the mix from the shaker into the glass.
Top op with soda water and decorate with cherries and a lemon peel twist.

Recommended: Copper Republic African Dry Gin.

Carlos Sainz: Driver and Strategist

Red Bull was ultimately dethroned when Ferrari's Carlos Sainz won the 2023 Singapore Grand Prix.

He did so in a sensible and cool manner, which helped McLaren's Lando Norris. Carlos did everything he could to win, even dropping back to give the pursuing McLaren driver DRS when the Mercedes cars closed in late in the race.

Carlos has always been a savvy driver, but this was especially stunning since it combined excellent strategy with his calm under severe pressure and heat to secure easily the best of his two F1 victories.

Closed circuit
Lap distance 5.513 km
Number of laps 56
Turns 20
DRS zones 2

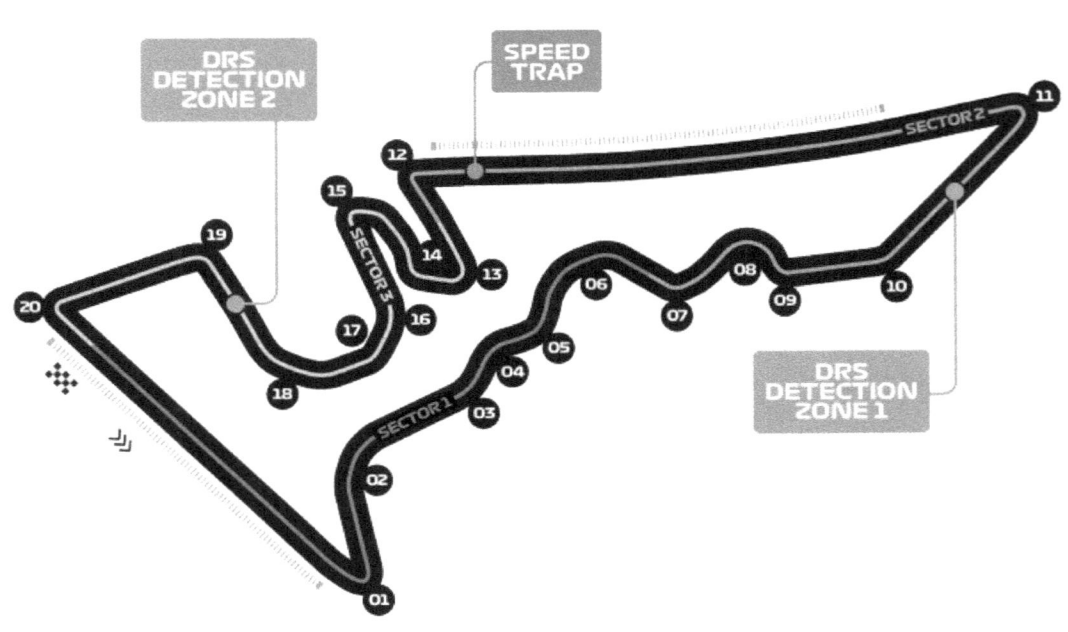

The Circuit of The Americas (COTA), designed by Hermann Tilke in collaboration with the American architectural firm HKS, had a rocky start, with several setbacks.

F1 returned to the Circuit of The Americas in 2012 for the first time since the Indianapolis Grand Prix in 2007.

Turns 3 to 6 are similar to Silverstone's high-speed run through Maggotts/Becketts or Suzuka's S Curves, while turns 12 to 15 are similar to Hockenheim's stadium section.

Meanwhile, the uphill run into wide turn 1 offers some excellent overtaking opportunities.

Road Runner

I might be showing my age when I say that my first encounter with a road runner was The Road Runner – the grey bird with the long neck, legs, and tail always being chased by Wile E. Coyote.

Well, these fast-running ground cuckoos are found in the southwestern and south-central regions of the US, including Texas.

60 ml gin
15 ml dry vermouth
15 ml Pernod anise liqueur
5 ml grenadine

Shake it all up over ice until well-chilled, then strain into a chilled wine glass.

Beep! Beep!

Recommended: Grey Hawk Gin.

Mexico City

Closed circuit

Lap distance 4.304 km

Number of laps 71

Turns 17

DRS zones 2

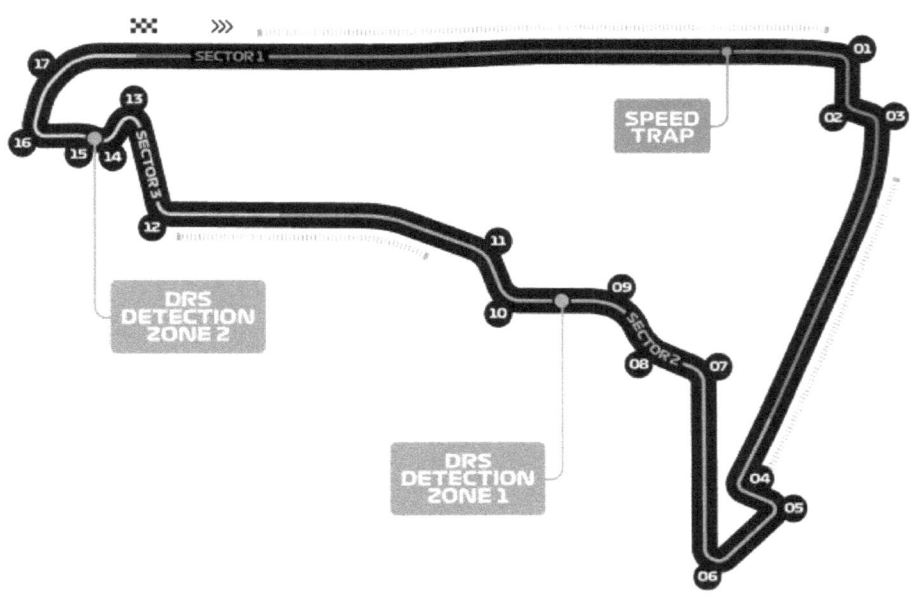

Formula 1 cars arrived in Mexico City in 1962 for a non-championship race before returning the following year for a proper Grand Prix. The Autodromo Hermanos Rodriguez is located more than two kilometres above sea level, making the 4.3 km lap an exhilarating experience. It can be difficult for teams to properly set up their cars to compensate for the thin air and avoid engine overheating.

Slow Comfortable Mexican Screw Against The Wall

"Slow" and "against the wall" are two things you definitely don't want to be in F1. This is a bit of a finicky one to build, but totally worth it.

20 ml tequila
20 ml vodka
90 ml orange juice
15 ml gin
15 ml vanilla liqueur

Add the first three ingredients into an ice-filled shaker and give it a quick shake before straining it into a highball glass.
Float˅ the gin onto the surface of mixed drink.
Then, float the vanilla liqueur on top of that. Garnish with an orange slice.

˅ To float an ingredient, slowly pour it over the back of a spoon held as close as possible to the surface of the liquid it is floated on top of.

Recommended: Two Gingers Spice Route Gin.

Rookie Driver Rule

Each F1 driver must give up a single FP1 session during the season to a super licence-holding rookie (a driver who has started two or fewer Grands Prix).

There is no regulation stating when this must happen, but most teams prefer to backload it. This is so they can get the most valuable information from experienced drivers at the start of the season for development. In addition, several of the F1 feeder championships have concluded by October or November, meaning the drivers are accessible.

Finally, the later in the year rookies race, the more spare components are available. So, often rookies will do their FP1 sessions with older-spec components.

Closed circuit

Lap distance 4.309 km

Number of laps 71

Turns 15

DRS zones 2

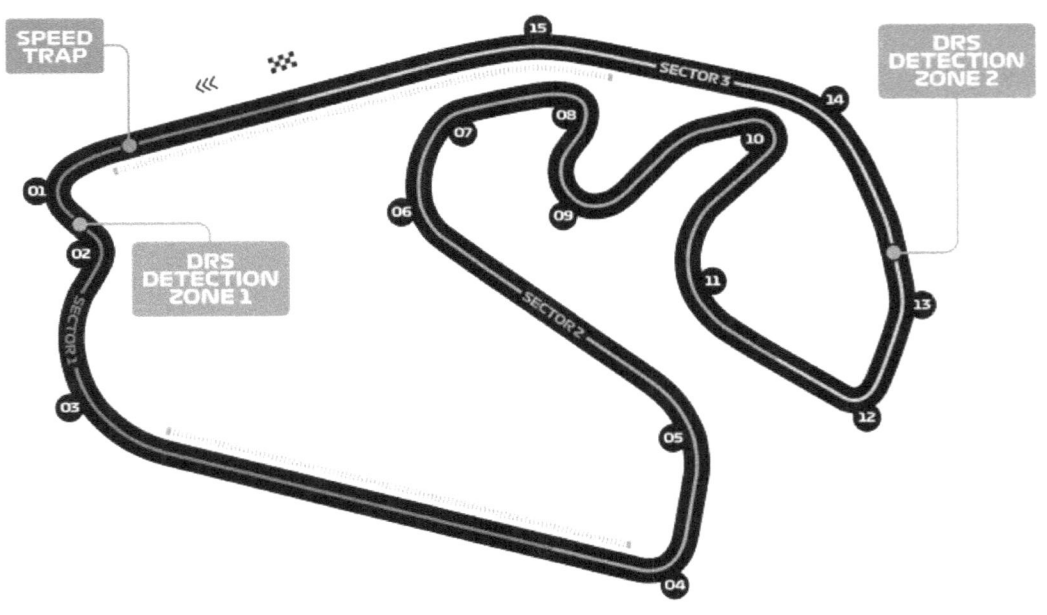

The Autódromo José Carlos Pace, also known as Interlagos, has witnessed some of the sport's most intense and bizarre spectacles.

Formula One arrived in Interlagos for the first time in 1973, buoyed by the success of Brazil's Emerson Fittipaldi. Interlagos, like many pre-World War II tracks, has banked corners, with drivers starting their lap on a sort of half oval.

After navigating the Senna S and down to turn 4, the drivers must navigate a snaking in-field section with some difficult camber changes before slinging back up the hill and through the banked final turn.

Gin Caipirinha

This zesty caipirinha recipe calls for gin instead of cachaça.

50 ml gin
½ lime cut into quarters
60 ml honey

Pop the lime wedges and honey into a shaker and muddle.
Add the gin and some ice before shaking well.
Pour – don't strain – everything into a rocks glass and garnish with a slice of lime.

Recommended: Knysna Honey Gin.

F1 Sprint Events

Sprint events were introduced into F1 in 2021 to spice up the action and ensure that each day of the racing weekend featured a competitive session: qualifying on Friday, sprint on Saturday, and grand prix on Sunday.

A sprint event is a race lasting only 100 kilometres. The winner receives eight points, second place receives seven points, and so on, down to eighth place with one point.

Sprint qualifying happens on Saturday mornings. Q1 lasts 12 minutes, Q2 10 minutes, and Q3 eight minutes, with seven-minute pauses in between. New tyres are required for each qualifying phase: medium tyres for Q1 and Q2, and soft tyres for Q3.

Street circuit
Lap distance 6.201 km
Number of laps 50
Turns 17
DRS zones 2

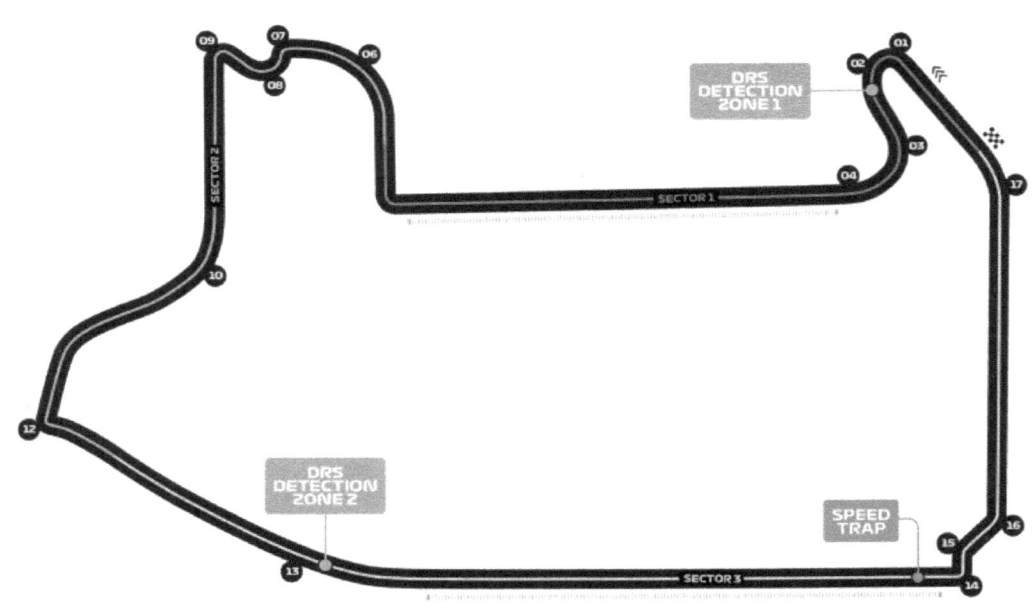

The Formula 1 Las Vegas Grand Prix 2023 was held on and around the Las Vegas Strip in Las Vegas, Nevada. The first Formula 1 race in Vegas was in 1981 at Caesars Palace so its return only took 40-odd years.

It is the second-longest street track behind the Jeddah Corniche Circuit. Overall, it is the second-longest track, with Belgium's Spa Francorchamps in first position.

After some controversy during the practice sessions in 2023, I think few fans or drivers would argue against it being one of the most enjoyable races of the season.

Tuxedo No. 2

I decided to go with a glamorous Vegas.

5 ml absinthe
75 ml gin
15 ml vermouth
7.5 ml maraschino liqueur
4 dashes orange bitters

Rinse your chilled cocktail glass with the absinthe. Discard any excess.
Add the rest of the ingredients into a mixing glass filled with ice and stir until chilled.
Strain into your prepared glass.
Garnish with a brandied cherry and orange twist.

Recommended: Native Gin.

Absinthe Rinse

Rinses are often used when you want a strong-flavoured ingredient like absinthe, to softly flavour your cocktail without dominating it. You're not adding alcohol to the drink with a rinse. Instead, you're adding scent and a faint flavour. Remember that up to 90% of what you perceive as flavour is actually aroma, and a wash can make a significant difference in the final drink.

Pour the absinthe into the chilled glass and swirl it around to coat the walls completely. Then, discard the absinthe and serve your cocktail. Alternatively, fill a spray bottle with absinthe and spritz the inside of your chilled glass a couple times before pouring in your cocktail for minimal waste.

Closed circuit

Lap distance 5.380 km

Number of laps 57

Turns 16

DRS zones 1

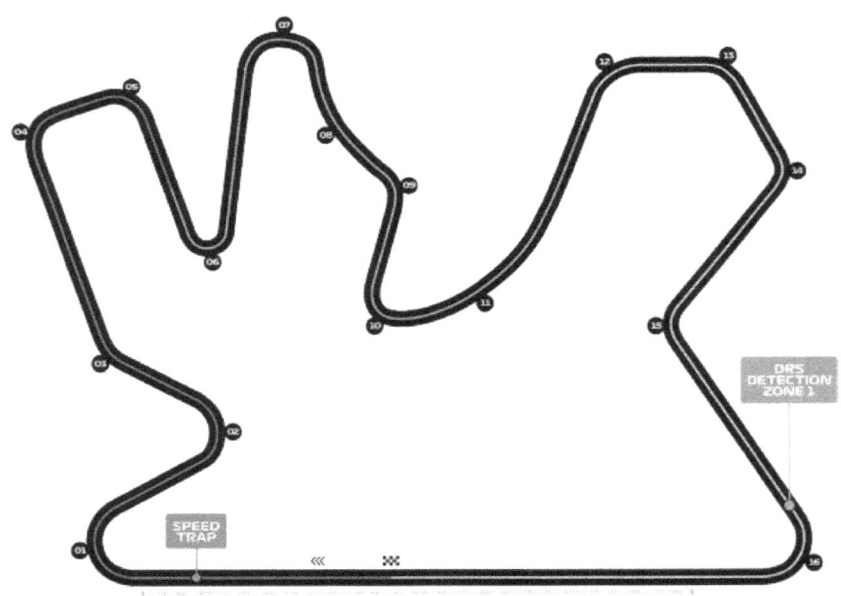

The Losail International Circuit was built primarily for motorcycle racing. The 5.4-kilometre track is fast and flowing, with medium- and high-speed corners dominating.

The track only has one straight, which is over one kilometre long and serves as the start grid, with plenty of overtaking opportunities into turn 1.

This cocktail is ideal for a night-time race and is perfect for wine lovers.

Moonlight

Serves four (4).

90 ml grapefruit juice
120 ml gin
30 ml kirsch
120 ml white wine
A pinch of lemon zest

Shake everything vigorously in a cocktail shaker filled with ice until chilled.
Strain into chilled couple glasses and garnish with a slice of lemon.

Recommended: Porkbush Gin.

Heat Exhaustion

The FIA said it is investigating methods to better prepare drivers for rising temperatures following the 2023 Qatar race.

Although the race began well after the sun had set, a 32-degree Celsius air temperature inside the cockpit climbed to over 49 degrees once the drivers got racing.

Lance Stroll said he was "passing out" and dizzy.

Esteban Ocon told media he vomited in his helmet.

Alexander Albon was checked by medical personnel for extreme heat exposure.

Logan Sargeant retired from the race after feeling ill and suffering from extreme dehydration.

Abu Dhabi (Yas Marina)

Closed circuit

Lap distance 5.281 km

Number of laps 58

Turns 16

DRS zones 2

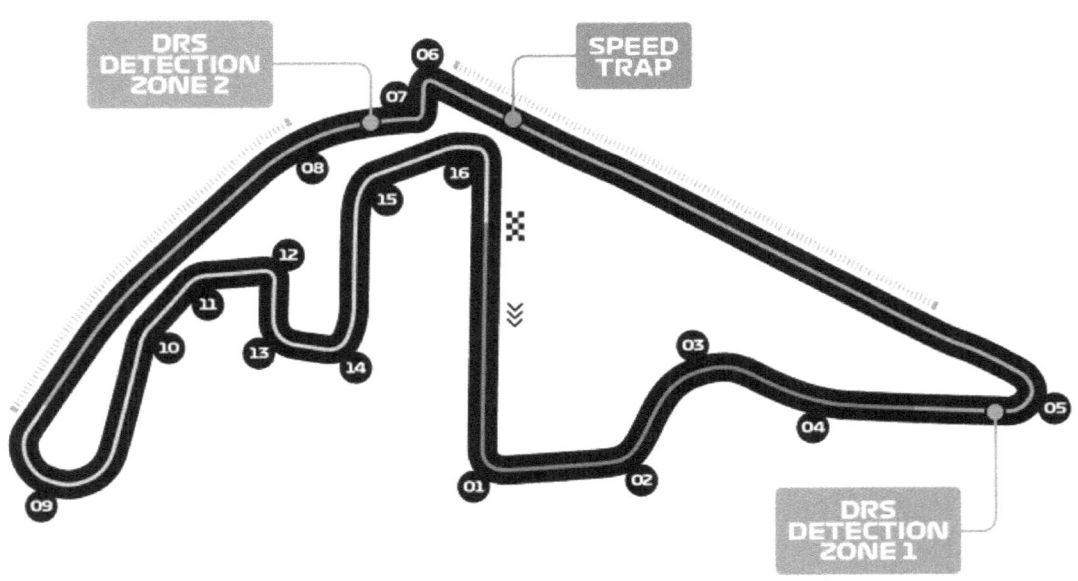

In 2006, plans were announced to develop Yas Island into a new tourist destination, with a racetrack at the centre of the plans. The track made its debut as the Formula 1 season finale in 2009.

The 1.2 km straight between turns 5 and 6 dominates the track, which, with slow-speed corners marking its beginning and end, makes it a haven for overtaking manoeuvres.

Other highlights include the tricky run through turns 10 and 11 into 12, which forces drivers to brake hard while carrying bags of lateral load.

G&C (Gin and Chai)

45 ml gin
10 ml chai syrup
20 ml lemon juice
Chilled champagne, prosecco or MCC

Shake the gin, chai syrup, and lemon juice with ice until well chilled.
Strain into a coupe glass and top up with the sparkling wine
Serve immediately.

Recommended: Sugarbird Safari Glitter Edition.

Acknowledgements

https://www.formula1.com/
https://www.hotcars.com/best-formula-1-race-tracks/
https://www.f1-fansite.com/
https://www.liquor.com/
https://www.planetsport.com/
https://www.thespruceeats.com/
https://f1.fandom.com/
https://www.cnbc.com/
https://www.motorsportmagazine.com/
https://www.planetf1.com/
https://www.motorsport.com/
Gin Shake, Muddle, Stir by Dan Jones
The Bartender's Guide to Gin
Kobus Bam and the team at
Right Click Media

Index of cocktails

Agua de Valencia

Bangkok G&T

Beach House

Bee's Knees

Blood & Sage

Classic G&T

Colt 45

Corpse Reviver No. 2

Dirty Martini

Earl Grey Marteani

Federal Ave. Swizzle

Firefly

French 75

G&C (Gin & Chai)

Gin & Earl Grey Bubble Tea

Gin & Juice – Lando's Version

Gin & Tequila Pineapple Punch

Gin Blossom
Gin Caipirinha
Gin Gimlet
Gin, Cherry & Apple Slushie
Ginger Roberts
Gin-Gin Mule
Great Dane
Lights Out Punch
Monte Carlo
Moonlight
Naked Peach
New Fashioned
Palm Beach
Pimms Cup
Pomegranate & Mint Shrub
Qui-Gon-Gin-Singer
Road Runner
Rosie Lee
Saketini
Silver Fizz

Singapore Sling
Slow Comfortable Mexican Screw Against The Wall
The Last Word
Timberpoint Cooler
Tom Collins Mocktail
Tuxedo No. 2
Valentino
Vesper

Index of gins

.L-Gin Lush
Autograph Gin
Belladonna Nightshade Gin
Black Rose Blush Gin
Blind Tiger Original Gin
Bloedlemoen Gin
Blossom & Hops Gin
Boplaas 8 Citrus Gin
Cape Saint Blaze Oceanic Gin
Cape Town Gin Classic Dry
Clemengold Gin
Copper Republic African Dry Gin
Cruxland Gin
D'Urban Barrel Aged Gin
Die Soet Rooinek Cherry Gin
Flowstone Wild Cucumber Gin
Geometric Gin

Gin Mare Mediterranean Gin
Ginologist Summer Cup
Grey Hawk Gin
Hope Navy Strength Gin
Inverroche Amber Gin
Jorgensen Pepper Gin
Knysna Honey Gin
Lieben Sailor Gin
Mirari Celebration Gin
Monk's Mary Jane Gin
Musgrave Original 11
Muti Gin
Native Gin
New Harbour Distillery Rooibos Gin
Pienaar & Son Orient Gin
Poetic Licence Northern Dry Gin
Porkbush Gin
Quince Classic Gin
Rhino Beetle Honey Gin

Seedlip Garden 108
Seedlip Grove 42
Six Dogs Honey Lime Gin
Still 33 Jenny Macadamia Nut Gin
Sugarbird Safari Glitter Edition
Triple Three Just Juniper Berry Gin
Two Gingers Spice Route Gin
Ugly Gin

www.ingramcontent.com/pod-product-compliance
Lightning Source LLC
Chambersburg PA
CBHW061756290426
44109CB00030B/2869